CONTENTS

Introduction

Growing up in India has had its fascinations, but almost nothing can equal a child's memory of meals had in the countryside kitchens of granny's home. Across the cool of mornings would echo the hooves of cattle let out to graze after they had been drained of their morning's supply of milk. As cauldrons of milk would be set on wood-fed stoves, the women of the house would bustle around churning buttermilk, adding dollops of butter to the previous night's leftover *rotis* or unleavened breads, or curds to the *khichra* or porridge of lentils and bajra. It was a robust meal with which to start the day.

Lunch was frugal, at least by city standards, consisting of freshly roasted bread and a chutney of garlic and chillies, washed down with buttermilk, though as a concession for us children visiting from the town, vegetables were specially prepared, to suit our sensitive stomachs.

Through the day, we would sneak into the storeroom next to granny's prayer room, where goodies were stored: *mishri* or crystallised sugar candy, pats of jaggery seasoned with aniseed, pickles, *ladoos* or balls of sweetmeats, *mathis* or unleavened patties without any stuffing, *shakarparas* or sugar coated flour biscuits, and the odd box of Mangharam biscuits in metal boxes with vividly coloured images of Bombay's Flora Fountain, almost as fascinating as the crinkly paper that lined its insides.

No one knew who these goodies were stored for: to the best of my knowledge, they were never served to members of the family, and we were the guests our grandparents had. Perhaps they were meant to be eaten the way we did—sneakily—adding a delicious layer of sin to our young appetites. Decades later, the pleasure of a forbidden meal or sweet remains far more exciting than the finest cordon bleu meal served openly, and with flourish, in the country's best restaurants.

The magic hours of dinner were unforgettable. *Shikar*, or hunting, was a sport cherished in our village, and it was not unusual to have a meal that consisted of partridge one night, hare another, venison a third night, to be followed the next day by imperial sandgrouse that migrated to the desert to escape the bone-chilling winter of Siberia. The kitchen inside the house, however, was *shudh*, literally pure or, in other words, vegetarian. Game, therefore, was cooked in the open, over a fire that was set into a pit. Here grandfather would sit, and it is the only time I remember him speaking directly to us. Having marinated his meats in *kachri*, a locally grown vegetable resembling a cucumber and which is used as a tenderiser, he would explain to us the merits of garlic, and how to be sure we browned the onions just right. The meat would then be roasted in the *masala* or spices till it was nearly done, and at this stage we were allowed a spoonful each in little bowls, and this semi-cooked food is the best I have ever tasted. Water would then be added, to make a curry and enough chillies added to sear the throat. Granny would send out chunky bajra rotis and a curry made of yoghurt and chickpea flour. And jugfuls of water. For we were eager to prove we were men, and how could a man spurn chillies?

Because my father was in the army, we travelled often, and all over India, and so began a journey that was linked by memorable repasts and feasts, parties and meals enjoyed in different homes, in different flavours. How different a *dal* or lentil curry could be in southern India with its vegetables, from that cooked in western India, which was sweetened with sugar. Or a dish of lamb, cooked in fat and chillies in Goa, curried in coconut in coastal India, tenderized with pomegranate in Hyderabad, or with papaya in north India, cooked with potatoes in Lucknow as stew, or pounded into a paste and garnished with raisins and almonds in Kashmir. Or take rice, eaten steamed or cooked with lemon curd, or made appetising with the addition of peas, or turned into a *biryani* (a rice preparation) flavoured with lamb or chicken, and garnished with saffron, and as *piece de resistance*, made into a *kheer* or porridge with cashewnuts and raisins and pistachios as India's simplest, but most popular, dessert.

As different as the variety of food itself, was the manner in which it was served. On banana leaves in the homes of the Chettinads of Tamil Nadu, or in temples and gurudwaras on Sundays. In *thaalis* or platters—of silver or bronze or steel—in which seven *katoris* or bowls of food would be placed along the rim, and a handful of rice along with accompaniments in the middle. Or in a formal table service, course by course, on china, using flatware and tableware that is a legacy of the two hundred years of British rule in India.

While regional availability of vegetables, fruits, spices and herbs have influenced the regional variations in Indian cuisine, without doubt the invasions the country has been subject to over centuries has added to its culinary repertoire. Here then are foods cooked in modest countryside homes, in extravagant palaces, in army camps, each of which has spawned its own style of cooking. Much of India's popular *tandoori* or barbecued food owes it culinary history to battle camps and the need to cook simply, without fuss. Which is why *tandoori* food depends so much on its marinades and spices, for, once basted and put into the tandoor or charcoal brazier, it was quickly roasted. As the story goes, a *nawab* (ruler) from Lucknow, passing by a great cauldron of mixed stew being cooked during a famine relief programme, inhaled the fragrance and spent the next years in creating a new cuisine—one of India's finest—called *dum pukht*. The Moghuls, as indeed the Muslims who preceded them into the country, enriched their curries with fruits and herbs that they brought with them from their mountain strongholds. The British combined the blandness of English cooking with the herbs found aplenty in India to create a school of Anglo-Indian cooking that still enjoys popularity in Calcutta, as does the one for fine confectioneries. The Parsis, the Portuguese, even the Dutch and the French, have left behind their imprints on Indian tastebuds, but never in isolation, for their tradition of cuisine has integrated with the Indian to create flavours as exotic on the palate as on the plate.

Not that this is a simple process, for the food habits of Indians are as complicated as their rituals and beliefs. More than half the nation is vegetarian due to religious beliefs. But just as the

Brahmins or priests shun meat, so too do the Kshatriyas or warriors extol its virtues. The Muslims eat beef but not pork, but the Hindus—those who are not vegetarian—eat pork but not beef. Some meat-eating communities do not eat fish for it is considered dirty, while other vegetarian communities do not mind fish, calling it but a vegetable of the sea because it is cold-blooded. Yet others do not eat brightly coloured vegetables, such as carrots or tomatoes, for they are supposed to excite passion, and for that very reason, the Jain community will not include onions and garlic in its diet.

Of such complexities and contradictions is the Indian table made, and it is this, perhaps, which is responsible for its astounding variety. Few Indian homes, be they so humble, will repeat a menu of vegetables or lentil curry more than once a week. A large number of festivals add their own repertoire with specialities and meals cooked for the occasion. And then there are foods meant for pregnant women and for new mothers, for young bridegrooms and for school-going children, enough, in fact, to ensure that anorexia could never take root in the land.

For a while, following the country's independence, as with much else in India, patronage was lost, and the Indian kitchen suffered a blow. Fortunately, recovery was quick, for the people whose families had served in the kitchens of royals and aristrocrats, merchants and masters, were still alive and able to impart what were traditional family secrets. From these recipes emerged the great Indian culinary revival, and the integration of culinary India.

In the absence of a restaurateur culture—till recently, Indians were loathe to eat out, and even now, the best Indian table will be found more in homes than in hotels—family chefs who had once served kings, began to work for hotels. Lost recipes were resurrected, and the great, grand tradition of Indian dining once again surfaced. No longer was it sufficient to qualify Indian cuisine by such generic terms as north Indian and south Indian. Regional specialities, community delicacies, were researched, and adapted to the modern palate, for the sedentary pace of life required adaptation. As utensils changed, and fuel changed, only one thing remained constant—the excellence of Indian dining.

It is such Master Chefs from the Ashok Group of Hotels who, over decades, in kitchens spread through the length and breadth of the country, have created a cuisine that is Indian, and yet belongs to the world. For the Ashok's Chefs have had the honour, as the official host to government functions, and the prime minister's banquets, to serve the best of India truly the way the world loves it. From Prime Minister Jawaharlal Nehru's interest in the kitchen to Indira Gandhi's close monitoring of the courses served to visiting dignitaries, to Rajiv Gandhi's introduction of nouvelle elements to Indian cuisine, to Narasimha Rao's insistence on a stronger southern 'representation' on the menu, the Chefs have journeyed across the vast culinary treasures of the country to serve only the finest gastronomic fare.

The Ashok's Chefs have accompanied Indian dignitaries overseas, played host to the world, cooked abroad the Queen Elizabeth cruise ship and at various international festivals. From these endeavours have been culled the recipes in this book, those that have an Indian identity and yet combine the basic ingredient with a primary spice or herb for flavour, to create a distinct taste for the tongue. A combination of these makes the most comprehensive Indian meal anyone is likely to have.

Typically, an Indian meal begins with a glass of buttermilk, or fresh lime soda, or even a soup served with a *pappadam*. The main course consists of rice or rotis or both, eaten with servings of vegetables, dal, a chicken or lamb curry, and curds. Accompaniments include a variety of pickles and chutneys, as well as salad. The meal is not served in courses, but together, so that the diner can savour different flavours simultaneously: sour, bitter, salty, sweet, pungent, spicy, hot.

And yet, despite its reputation, curry is not the only Indian dish you will know. In fact, curry, in India means gravy. A standard food called curry does not exist. For a curry could be vegetarian or non-vegetarian. It could be coconut-flavoured, or bitter with asafoetida. It could be cooked with yoghurt, or in cashewnuts. It could be chilli or sweet. If you were to ask for 'curry' in India, a waiter might at first look dazed, then proceed to rattle off hundreds of names of dishes you would never have thought existed. Such as raw bananas cooked in masala, or prawns in a coconut gravy, or corn bread eaten with spinach. Or lotus stems put into a curry, or lotus seeds roasted to airy lightness and used to make a milk-dessert. Of course, there are hundreds of Indian sweetmeat—probably the largest in the world—and mouth-watering delicacies that can be eaten before, after, during or in place of a meal. And at the end of it all, condiments and *paans* (betel leaf), to cleanse the mouth and aid the digestive process.

Snacking has such exciting components as *samosas* (conical pastries stuffed with spicy potatoes), *dosas* or pancakes served with a coconut chutney, a host of kababs or barbecued meats, *bhelpuri* or puffed rice made exciting with groundnuts, chopped onions and tomatoes—and green chillies: and *chaat*, an exciting amalgamation of crisp *paparis* (fried pastry rounds) served with potatoes, grams, and layered with mint and tamarind chutneys and curds.

As the palate explores different tastes, it is time to go down memory lane once more, to feasts remembered, and India's great recipes that make Indian cooking among the best in the world.

Kishore Singh

Raee (Mustard) Seeds

Tej Patta (Bay Leaves)

Star Anise

Choti Elaichi (Green Cardamom)

Kalonji (Onion) Seeds

Saunf (Fennel) Seeds

Sonth (Dry Ginger)

Javitri (Mace)

Bari Elaichi (Black Cardamom)

Methi Dana (Fenugreek Seeds)

Kali Mirch (Black Pepper Corns)

Red Chillies, whole

Daalchini (Cinnamon)

Dhania (Coriander) Seeds

Zeera (Cumin) Seeds

Ajwain (Carom) Seeds

Laung (Cloves)

Jaiphal (Nutmeg)

Khus Khus
(Poppy
seeds)

Kala Namak
(Black Rock Salt)

Sonth (Dry
Ginger)
Powder

Lal Mirch
(Red Chilli)
Powder

Chaat
Masala

Sambhar Powder

Kasoori Methi (Dry
Fenugreek) Powder

White Pepper
Powder

Amchoor
(Dry
Mango)
Powder

Dhania (Coriander)
Powder

Haldi
(Turmeric)
Powder

Zeera (Cumin) Powder

Heeng (Asafoetida)
Powder

Namak
(Salt)

Garam Masala

Til (Sesame)
Seeds

Garam
Masala

Onions,
browned

Ginger
Paste

Garlic Paste

Khoya

Cottage Cheese
(Paneer)

Onion
Paste

Tomato
Purée

Basic Indian Recipes

Ginger Paste:
Soak ginger (250 gms) overnight to soften the skin. Peel and chop roughly. Process until pulped, using very little water if required. The plup can be stored in an air tight container and refrigerated for 4-6 weeks

Garlic Paste:
Soak garlic (250 gms) overnight to soften the skin. Peel the garlic cloves and chop roughly. Process until pulped, using very little water if required. The pulp can be stored in an air tight container and refrigerated for 4-6 weeks.

Onion Paste:
Peel and chop the onions (500 gms) into quarters. Process until pulped, using very little water if required. The pulp can be stored in an air tight container and refrigerated for 4-6 weeks.

Brown Onion Paste:
Slice the onions (500 gms) and fry over medium heat until brown. Remove, drain excess oil and allow to cool. Process until pulped, using very little water if required. The pulp can be stored in an air tight container and refrigerated for 4-6 weeks.

Paneer (cottage cheese):
In a pot, put milk (3 litres) to boil. Just before it boils add lemon juice or white vinegar (60 ml / 4 tbs) to curdle the milk. Strain the curdled milk through a muslin cloth to allow all whey and moisture to drain. Allow to hang under a weight for 2-3 hours to set in a block which can be cut or grated.

Khoya:
Boil full cream milk (2 litres) in a kadhai (wok), reduce heat to low and boil till the milk is reduced to half, stirring occassionally. Continue cooking, now, stirring constantly and scrapping from the sides till a thick paste-like consistency is obtained (1-1 1/2 hours). Allow to cool and refrigerate. Use as required.

Onions, browned:
Peel and slice 2 large onions. Heat oil in a kadhai (wok) and fry the sliced onions on medium heat until golden brown. Remove and drain excess oil. Use immediately for garnishing any dish.

Tomato Purée:
Peel and chop the tomatoes (1 kg), remove the seeds. In a pan, cook the tomatoes on medium heat alongwith Water (1 litre), Cloves 8, Green cardamoms 8, Ginger 15 gms, Garlic 10 gms, Bayleaves 5 and Black peppercorns 5 gms, until the tomatoes are tender. Remove from heat, allow to cool and process until pulped. Can be stored in an air tight container and refrigerated for 4-6 weeks.

Garam Masala:
450 gms, broil the following ingredients in a thick bottomed pan. Cumin seeds (200 gms), Black pepper corns (35 gms), Black cardamom seeds (45 gms), Green cardamom (30 gms), Coriander seeds (60 gms), Cloves (20 gms), Cinnamom sticks (20 gms), Mace powder (20 gms), Bayleaves (15 gms), Ginger powder (30 gms), Nutmeg (2). Allow to cool and grind to a powder. Store in an air tight container and use as required.

SOUPS & JUICES

Clockwise from left: Tomato and Coconut Soup, Palak Shorba and Carrot and Orange Soup (page 19). Dahi Shorba, Tomato and Coriander Soup (page 17). Watermelon Juice, Bel ka Sharbat and Tender Coconut Shikanji (page 21), Haleem Shorba (page 23).

Cold Cucumber Soup

Green Cucumber blended with cream, served chilled

Serves: 4, Preparation time: 30 minutes, Cooking time: 45 minutes

Ingredients:

Cucumber,quartered alongwith peel .... *1 kg*
Butter .... *25 gms / 5 tsp*
Onions, quartered .... *200 gms / 1 cup*
Vegetable stock, strained .... *2 litres / 10 cups*

Salt to taste
White pepper powder .... *3 gms / ½ tsp*
Cream, whipped .... *100 gms / ½ cup*

Method:

1. Heat butter in a pot, add onions and sauté till transparent, add the cucumber and sauté for a few minutes.
2. Stir in the veg.stock, salt to taste and white pepper powder. Cover and cook on low heat for 20-25 minutes till the cucumber is cooked and tender. Stir in the cream,

remove from heat and allow to cool.
3. Blend the soup to obtain a purée and strain through a muslin cloth.
4. Transfer to a soup bowl and refrigerate for 1 hour.
5. Serve chilled, garnished with cream. (Picture on page 15).

Dahi Shorba

Tangy yoghurt soup

Serves: 4, Preparation time: 15 minutes, Cooking time: 25 minutes

Ingredients:

Yoghurt .... *300 gms / 1½ cups*
Butter .... *25 gms / 5 tbs*
Fenugreek *(methi)* seeds .... *10 gms / 2 tsp*
Mustard *(raee)* seeds .... *10 gms / 2 tsp*
Gramflour *(besan)* .... *150 gms / ¾ cup*
Salt to taste
White pepper powder .... *5 gms / 1 tsp*

Turmeric *(haldi)* powder .... *5 gms / 1 tsp*
White Radish, peeled, cut into cubes .... *225 gms / 1 cup*
Water .... *3 lt / 15 cups*
Curry leaves .... *10 gms / 2 tsp*
Curry powder .... *5 gms / 1 tsp*
Cream .... *100 gms / ½ cup*

Method:

1. Melt butter in a pot, add fenugreek and mustard seeds, sauté till they crackle, add gramflour, salt, white pepper powder, turmeric powder, and radish blended in yoghurt.
2. Add water (1 litre / 5 cups) and cook till a pleasing smell of gramflour emanates. Reduce heat and simmer for

10 minutes.
3. Add the remaining water and curry leaves, cook on low heat till it comes to a boil. Stir in the curry powder.
4. Remove from heat and pass through a soup strainer.
5. Stir in the cream, transfer to soup bowls and serve.

Tomato and Coriander Soup

Cream of tomato braised with coriander

Serves: 4, Preparation time: 15 minutes, Cooking time: 35 minutes

Ingredients:

Tomatoes, chopped .... *500 gms / 2½ cups*
Butter .... *30 gms / 2 tbs*
Coriander seeds .... *2 gms / ⅓ tsp*
Ginger, chopped .... *5 gms / 1 tsp*
Garlic, chopped .... *5 gms / 1 tsp*
Flour .... *40 gms / 2 ⅔ tbs*

Bayleaves *(tej patta)* *4*
Salt .... *15 gms / 1 tbs*
White pepper powder .... *3 gms / ½ tsp*
Vegetable stock .... *1½ litre / 7 cups*
Orange/Red colour .... *5 gms / 1 tsp*
Green coriander, chopped .... *20 gms / 4 tsp*

Method:

1. Melt butter in a handi *(pot)*, add coriander seeds and sauté till they crackle. Add ginger and garlic and sauté for a minute.
2. Add flour and cook to a sandy texture without colouring, add the tomatoes and sauté for a few minutes.
3. Stir in the remaining ingredients except green coriander

and cook for about 20 minutes.
4. Remove from heat and pass through a soup strainer.
5. Add the green coriander and reheat till it comes to a boil.
6. Remove from heat and transfer to soup bowls.
7. Serve immediately, garnished with green coriander.

Tomato and Coconut Soup

Tomato soup laced with coconut milk

Serves: 4, Preparation time: 15 minutes, Cooking time: 30 minutes

Ingredients:

Tomatoes,chopped .... 500 gms / 2 ½ cups	Salt to taste
Coconut, grated .... 100 gms / ½ cup	White pepper powder .... 2 gms / ¹/3 tsp
Coconut oil .... 40 ml / 2 ²/3 tbs	Bayleaves *(tej patta)* 4
Garlic, chopped.................................... 10 gms / 2 tsp	Vegetable stock .... 1 ½ litres / 7 cups
Onions, chopped .... 50 gms / 3 ¹/3 tbs	Cream .... 40 gms / 2 ²/3 tbs
Ginger, crushed.................................... 15 gms / 1 tbs	

Method:

1. Heat coconut oil in a pot. Sauté garlic and onions for a few seconds.
2. Add coconut and stir-fry. Add tomatoes and ginger.
3. Stir in the salt, white pepper powder, bayleaves and vegetable stock. Allow to simmer for 15-20 minutes till the tomatoes are cooked and tender.

4. Remove from heat and allow to cool.
5. Blend to obtain a purée, strain through a muslin cloth and reheat.
6. Remove from heat and stir in the cream.
7. Transfer to soup bowl and serve immediately.

Palak Shorba

Cumin and garlic flavoured veloute of spinach

Serves: 4, Preparation time: 20 minutes, Cooking time: 30 minutes

Ingredients:

Spinach *(palak)* .... 500 gms / 2 ½ cups	Black peppercorns .... 2 gms / ¹/3 tsp
Butter .... 30 gms / 2 tbs	Bayleaves *(tej patta)* 4
Flour.. 30 gms / 2 tbs	Salt to taste
Ginger, chopped .... 25 gms / 5 tsp	White pepper powder .... a pinch
Garlic, chopped................................... 5 gms / 1 tsp	Vegetable stock .... 1 ½ litres / 7 cups

Method:

1. Chop the spinach leaves into small pieces and wash thoroughly.
2. Melt buttter in a handi *(pot)*. Add flour and cook to a sandy texture.
3. Add ginger, garlic, spinach and sauté for a few minutes. Add black peppercorns and bayleaves.
4. Stir in the salt, white pepper powder and vegetable

stock. Simmer for 15-20 minutes.
5. Remove the spinach from the stock and blend to a purée. Return the spinach purée to the stock and cook for 5 minutes.
6. Remove from heat, transfer to soup bowls and serve hot.

Carrot and Orange Soup

Puréed carrots blended with orange juice, served hot

Serves: 4, Preparation time: 1 hour, Cooking time: 40 minutes

Ingredients:

Carrots, cut into small cubes .... 500 gms / 2 ½ cups	White pepper powder .... 2 gms / ¹/3 tsp
Orange juice .... 800 ml / 4 cups	Sugar .... 50 gms / 3 ¹/3 tbs
Butter .... 25 gms / 5 tsp	Cream .... 100 gms / ½ cup
Onions, chopped .... 150 gms / ²/3 cup	
Salt to taste	

Method:

1. Heat butter in a pan, add the onion and sauté till transparent.
2. Add the carrots and sauté for a minute. Add the remaining ingredients except cream and cook on low heat till the carrot pieces are tender.

3. Remove and pass through a soup strainer and then strain through a muslin cloth.
4. Reheat the strained soup and stir in the cream.
5. Remove from heat and transfer to soup bowls.
6. Serve hot.

Watermelon Juice

A delightful blend of watermelon with a touch of mint

Serves: 4, Preparation time: 30 minutes

Ingredients:

Watermelons .... *4.5 kgs*
Mint leaves, chopped .... *5 gms / 1 tsp*

Black rock salt *(kala namak)* to taste

Method:

1. Cut the flesh into small chunks and discard the rind.
2. Remove all the seeds, put in a mixie bowl with mint leaves.
3. Blend to make a purée.

4. Pass through a muslin cloth, discard the waste.
5. Chill in a refrigerator.
6. Pour into glasses and serve.

Bel ka Sharbat

Wood Apple Squash, a summer time favourite of all.

4 portions, Preparation time: 8-10 hours

Ingredients:

Bel *(large)* *1*
Water .... *1 litre / 5 cups*

Sugar, powdered .... *100 gms / ½ cup*

Method:

1. Break open the bel and remove the pulp.
2. Soak the pulp in water and leave to rest overnight.
3. Dissolve sugar in the bel water and strain through a

muslin cloth.
4. Chill in a refrigerator.
5. Pour into serving glass and serve.

Tender Coconut Shikanji

Ginger blended coconut water with a touch of lemon

Serves:4, Preparation time: 30 minutes.

Ingredients:

Green or Tender coconuts *4*
Sugar, powdered .... *150 gms / ¾ cup*

Lemon *3*
Ginger juice, strained .... *10 ml / 2 tsp*

Method:

1. Extract the water from the coconuts.
2. Dissolve sugar in the coconut water. Add juice of 3 lemons and ginger. Strain through a muslin cloth.

3. Chill in a refrigerator.
4. Pour to serving glasses and serve.

Broccoli and Walnut Soup

Creamed broccoli served with walnuts

Serves: 4, Preparation time: 15 minutes, Cooking time: 40 minutes

Ingredients:

Broccoli, florets only .... *400 gms / 2 cups*
Walnuts, chopped .... *16 gms / 1 tbs*
Butter .... *30 gms / 2 tbs*
Onions, chopped .... *30 gms / 2 tbs*
Garlic, chopped.. *5 gms / 1 tsp*
Leeks, chopped .... *20 gms / 4 tsp*

Celery, chopped .... *20 gms / 4 tsp*
Salt to taste
White pepper powder .... *2 gms / ⅓ tsp*
Vegetable stock .... *1 ½ litres / 7 cups*
Cream .... *100 gms / ½ cup*

Method:

1. Heat butter in a handi *(pot)*. Add onions and garlic, sauté for a minute. Add leeks, celery, broccoli, and stir-fry.
2. Stir in salt, white pepper powder and veg. stock. Simmer for 20 minutes until the broccoli is tender.
3. Remove the broccoli from the soup, allow to cool and

blend to a purée. Mix the purée into the soup, strain through a muslin cloth.
4. Reheat the strained soup and stir in the cream.
5. Remove from heat, transfer to soup bowls and serve hot, garnished with walnuts.

Rasam

Spicy and tangy lentil soup

Serves:4, Preparation time: 30-40 minutes, Cooking time:40 minutes.

Ingredients:

Lentils *(arhar daal)* .... 100 gms / ½ cup	Ginger, chopped .... 13 gms / 2 ⅓ tsp
Tamarind *(imli)* .... 40 gms / 2 ⅔ tsp	Black peppercorns .... 6 gms / 1 tsp
Turmeric *(haldi)* powder .... 6 gms / 1 tsp	Asafoetida *(heeng)* ....3 gms / ½ tsp
Red chilli powder................................... 8 gms / 1 ½ tsp	Water.. 1 litre / 5 cups
Salt .... 16 gms / 1tbs	**For the tempering:**
Coriander powder .... 16 gms / 1 tbs	Red chillies, whole .... 3 gms / ½ tsp
Tomatoes, quartered .... 160 gms / ¾ cup	Mustard *(raee)* seeds .... 8 gms / 1 ½ tsp
Cumin *(jeera)* seeds, powdered.............. 8 gms / 1 ½ tsp	Sesame *(til)* seeds .... 5 gms / 1 tsp
Garlic, chopped .... 8 gms / 1 ½ tsp	Curry leaves .... 1 sprig

Method:

1. Soak tamarind in water, squeeze out the pulp and discard waste.

2. Soak lentils in water for ½ hour. Drain and keep aside.

3. Heat the tamarind extract in a handi *(pot)*, add turmeric powder, red chilli powder, salt, coriander powder and tomatoes and cook on low heat for 20 minutes.

4. Add cumin, garlic, ginger, black peppercorns and asafoetida, mix well and cook for another 10 minutes.

5. Stir in the lentils alongwith water. Bring to a boil, reduce heat and cook for 10 minutes. Remove from heat and pass through a soup strainer.

6. For the tempering, heat oil in a pan, add red chillies, mustard seeds, sesame seeds and curry leaves. Sauté till they crackle.

7. Remove from heat and add this to the prepared soup.

8. Serve hot, as a starter or as an accompaniment to a meal.

Salted Lassi

Salted butter milk

Serves: 4, Preparation time: 15 minutes.

Ingredients:

Yoghurt .... 1 kg	Salt .... 15 gms / 1 tbs
Water.. 400 ml / 2 cups	Ice cubes .... 200 gms / 1 cup

Method:

1. Mix yoghurt alongwith water, salt and ice cubes until thoroughly mixed.

2. Pour into serving glasses.

3. Serve cold, as a starter or an accompaniment to a meal.

Haleem Shorba

Lamb broth laced with wheat milk

Serves: 4, Preparation time: 12-14 hours, Cooking time: 5 hours

Ingredients:

Lamb, bones .... 1 kg	White butter.. 50 gms / 3 ⅓ tbs
Wheat.. 100 gms / ½ cup	Onions, chopped .... 50 gms / 3 ⅓ tbs
Water.. 2 litres / 10 cups	Almond paste .... 50 gms / 3 ⅓ tbs
Garam masala, whole .... 10 gms / 2 tsp	Salt to taste	
Bayleaf *(tej patta)* 1	White pepper powder .... 3 gms / ½ tsp
Onions, pounded .... 10 gms / 2 tsp	Saffron *(kesar)* .... a few strands
Garlic, chopped .... 10 gms / 2 tsp	**For garnishing:**
Ginger, chopped .... 10 gms / 2 tsp	Lamb brunoise, boiled .... 50 gms / 3 ⅓ tbs

Method:

1. Soak wheat in sufficient water overnight and squeeze out the wheat milk.

2. Heat water (2 litres / 10 cups) in a handi *(pot)*, add the lamb bones, garam masala, bayleaf, onion, garlic, ginger and allow to cook for about 4-5 hours on low heat. Remove from heat and strain through a soup strainer.

3. Melt butter in a pan and sauté the onions till slightly

browned. Stir in the strained stock, cook for 5-10 minutes.

4. Add the almond paste and allow to cook for 5 minutes. Stir in the salt and white pepper powder. Remove from heat and strain the stock.

5. Reheat the stock in a handi *(pot)*, add saffron and wheat milk. Bring to a boil and remove from heat.

6. Serve hot, garnished with boiled lamb brunoise. (Picture on page 15).

CHICKEN

Clockwise from left: Murg Daraanpur (page 29), Chicken Badam Pasanda (page 31), Tandoori Kofta (page 33) and Murg Jugalbandi (page 35).

Murg Kandhari

Chicken cooked with pomegranate juice

Serves: 4, Preparation time: 20 minutes, Cooking time: 25 minutes

Ingredients:

Chicken, cut into boneless pieces	700 gms	Water	200 ml / 1 cup
Ginger-garlic paste *(page 13)*	15 gms / 1 tbs	Brown onion paste *(page 13)*	20 gms / 4 tsp
Salt	8 gms / 1 ½ tsp	Tomato purée *(page 13)*	40 gms / 2 ⅔ tbs
Red chilli powder	4 gms / ¾ tsp	Pomegranate *(anardana)* seeds	100 gms / ½ cups
Oil	40 ml / 2 ⅔ tbs	Cream	50 gms / 3 ⅓ tbs
Cashewnut paste	60 gms / 4 tbs	Garam masala *(page 13)*	3 gms / ½ tsp
Yoghurt	50 gms / 3 ⅓ tbs		

Method:

1. Wash, clean and dry the chicken pieces. Marinate the chicken pieces with ginger-garlic paste (2 tsp), half of salt and red chilli powder and keep aside for 10-15 minutes.

2. Heat oil (30 ml) in a pan. Sauté the chicken pieces for a few minutes without letting the colour change. Keep aside.

3. Add the remaining oil to the pan, sauté the remaining ginger-garlic paste for 2-3 minutes. Add cashewnut paste mixed with yoghurt and water. Season with remaining salt and red chilli powder, simmer for 8-10 minutes.

4. Add the brown onion paste, tomato purée and chicken pieces and cook on low heat till the chicken is tender and the curry has thickened.

5. Extract juice from pomegranate seeds and strain through a muslin cloth into the simmering curry.

6. Stir in the cream. Remove from heat, transfer to a serving dish, and serve hot, garnished with garam masala.

Chicken Bannu Kabab

A delicate kabab of chicken cubes with a hint of fenugreek

Serves: 4, Preparation time: 45 minutes, Cooking time: 20 minutes

Ingredients:

Chicken, cut into boneless cubes	900 gms	Vinegar	5 gms / 1 tsp
Salt	10 gms / 2 tsp	Oil	70 gms / 4 ⅔ tbs
Dry fenugreek *(kasoori methi)* powder	2 gms / ⅓ tsp	Gramflour *(besan)*, seived	25 gms / 5 tsp
Ginger-garlic paste *(page 13)*	30 gms /2 tbs	Bread crumbs, fresh	40 gms / 2 ⅔ tbs
Green chillies, chopped	10 gms / 2 tsp	Egg *(yolks only)*, whisked	6
Green coriander, chopped	10 gms /2 tsp		

Method:

1. Wash and dry the chicken cubes. Add salt, dry fenugreek powder, ginger-garlic paste, green chillies, green coriander alongwith vinegar to the cubes and mix thoroughly. Refrigerate for 15 minutes.

2. Heat oil in a pan, add gramflour and stir-fry till a pleasing smell emanates. Add the chicken cubes and sauté on low heat for 3-5 minutes till they are half cooked.

3. Add breadcrumbs and mix well. Remove and spread on a clean table top. Allow to cool.

4. Skewer the cubes 2" apart and roast in a tandoor till done. Bring the cubes close together and coat with egg yolks.

5. Roast in the tandoor till the egg yolk coating turns golden brown in colour. Remove from the skewer and serve hot, garnished with onion rings and accompanied by Mint chutney (page 91). (Picture on page 24).

Neza Kabab

Marinated chicken legs with a distinctive flavour of green cardamom

Serves: 4, Preparation time: 40 minutes, Cooking time: 25 minutes

Ingredients:

Chicken, legs .... *900 gms*	Green coriander, chopped .... *40 gms / 2 2/3 tbs*
Ginger-garlic paste *(page 13)* .... *80 gms / 5 1/3 tbs*	Green cardamom *(choti elaichi)* powder . *4 gms / 3/4 tsp*
Salt .... *8 gms / 1 1/2 tsp*	Oil .... *60 ml / 4 tbs*
White pepper powder .... *4 gms / 3/4 tsp*	Gramflour *(besan)* .... *300 gms / 1 1/2 cups*
Garam masala *(page 13)* .... *4 gms / 3/4 tsp*	Eggs, whisked *4*
Dry fenugreek *(kasoori methi)* powder ..... *2 gms / 1/3 tsp*	Cream .... *200 gms / 1 cup*
Vinegar .... *20 ml / 4 tsp*	Butter for basting

Method:

1. Wash and clean the chicken legs. Remove the thigh bone from the flesh. Take care to see that it is not completely removed.

2. Prepare a marinade by mixing together ginger-garlic paste, salt, white pepper powder, garam masala, dry fenugreek powder, vinegar, green coriander and green cardamom powder. Marinate the chicken legs in this marinade and keep aside for 20 minutes.

3. Heat oil in a pan, add gramflour and stir-fry on low heat till a pleasing smell emanates. Remove from heat and transfer to a mixing bowl and allow to cool.

4. Add 1 egg and blend to make a smooth paste, add cream and mix well.

5. Add the remaining eggs to the mixture and mix thoroughly. Coat the chicken legs with this marinade and keep aside for 20 minutes.

6. Skewer the chicken legs once along the bone and once through the thigh flesh. Cook in a tandoor for about 8-10 minutes or till slightly coloured. Remove and let excess liquids drip.

7. Baste lightly with butter and roast again for 2-3 minutes or till completely done.

8. Remove from skewers onto a serving platter, garnish with lemon wedges, cucumber and tomato dices, onion rings and serve hot.

Murg Daraanpur

Chicken breasts coated with cornflour mixture and deep fried

Serves: 4, Preparation time: 1 hour, Cooking time: 20-30 minutes

Ingredients:

Chicken, breasts *8*	Cashewnuts, chopped .... *50 gms / 3 1/3 tbs*
Red chilli powder .... *4 gms / 3/4 tsp*	Green coriander, chopped .... *12 gms / 2 1/3 tsp*
Garam masala *(page 13)* .... *2 gms / 1/3 tsp*	Green chillies, chopped .... *10 gms / 2 tsp*
Dry fenugreek *(kasoori methi)* powder .... *a pinch*	**For the batter:**
White pepper powder .... *a pinch*	Cornflour .... *100 gms / 1/2 cup*
Salt .... *3 gms / 1/2 tsp*	Water .... *300 ml / 1 1/2 cups*
Ginger-garlic paste *(page 13)* .... *16 gms / 1 tbs*	Vinegar .... *5 ml / 1 tsp*
Vinegar .... *5 ml / 1 tsp*	Salt .... *a pinch*
Oil .... *10 ml / 2 tsp*	White pepper powder .... *a pinch*
For the filling:	Flour... *65 gms / 4 1/3 tbs*
Cheese, grated .... *600 gms / 3 cups*	Ginger-garlic paste *(page 13)* .... *8 gms / 1 1/2 tsp*
Chicken tikka, cooked, chopped .... *190 gms*	Eggs, whisked *2*
Raisins, chopped .... *50 gms / 3 1/3 tbs*	Oil for frying

Method:

1. Wash, clean and dry the chicken breasts.

2. Mix together red chilli powder, garam masala, dry fenugreek powder, white pepper powder, salt, ginger-garlic paste, vinegar and oil to make a paste.

3. Slit the chicken breasts from the sides, open out and flatten with a steak hammer without rupturing the flesh.

4. Smear the chicken breasts with the prepared paste evenly.

5. Prepare the filling, by mixing together cheese, chicken tikka, raisins, cashewnuts, green coriander and green chillies.

6. Divide the filling into 8 equal portions and place in the centre of each piece.

7. Roll the pieces firmly over the filling and refrigerate for 10 minutes.

8. Dissolve the cornflour in water to a lump free batter, add vinegar, salt, white pepper powder, flour, ginger-garlic paste and eggs. Mix well.

9. Heat oil in a kadhai *(wok)*, dip each chicken piece in the cornflour batter and deep fry on medium hot oil till half done.

10. Remove and drain excess oil.

11. Just before serving, deep fry the pieces 'daraanpur' until golden brown in colour, remove, cut into half and serve. (Picture on page 25).

Chooza Kabab

Skewered chicken chunks in a highly aromatic and flavourful curry,
served with capsicum and onions on a bed of rice

Serves: 4, Preparation time: 45 minutes, Cooking time: 15 minutes

Ingredients:

Chicken, cut into boneless pieces .... 900 gms	Cinnamon *(daalchini)* sticks 2
Basmati rice .... 300 gms / 1 ½ cup	Cloves *(laung)* 2
Yoghurt .... 10 gms / 2 tsp	Bayleaves *(tej patta)* 4
Ginger-garlic paste *(page 13)* .... 30 gms / 2 tbs	Brown onion paste *(page 13)* .... 125 gms / ½ cup
Salt to taste	Dry coconut, grated .... 35 gms / 2 ⅓ tbs
Curry powder .... 10 gms / 2 tsp	Turmeric *(haldi)* powder .... 10 gms / 2 tsp
Tomatos, quartered .... 235 gms / 1⅓ cup	Red chilli powder .... 3 gms / ½ tsp
Onions, quartered .... 145 gms / ¾ cup	Coriander powder .... 15 gms / 1 tbs
Capsicum, quartered .... 90 gms / 6 tbs	Tomato purée *(page 13)* .... 100 gms / ½ cup
Oil .... 80 ml / 5⅓ tbs	Chicken stock .... 500 ml / 2 ½ cups
Cumin *(jeera)* seeds .... 2 gms / ⅓ tsp	Cream .... 60 gms / 4 tbs
Black cardamom *(bari elaichi)* 2	Green coriander, chopped .... 20 gms / 4 tsp
Green cardamom *(choti elaichi)* 2	

Method:

1. Marinate the chicken pieces in yoghurt, ginger-garlic paste (2 tsp), salt (½ tsp), curry powder (½ tsp) and oil (1 tsp). Keep aside for 20 minutes.

2. Clean and soak the rice in water for 20 minutes. Boil in sufficient water until cooked. Remove and keep aside.

3. Skewer the marinated chicken pieces in alternate layers with tomato, onion and capsicum quarters and grill over a hot plate till completely cooked from all sides, basting with oil from time to time. Remove & keep aside.

4. For the curry, heat oil (3⅓ tbs) in a pan, add cumin seeds, black cardamom, green cardamom, cinnamon, cloves and bayleaves, saute till they crackle.

5. Stir in the remaining ginger-garlic paste and sauté further for a minute. Add brown onion paste, coconut, turmeric powder, red chilli powder, coriander powder and remaining curry powder. Stir-fry till the oil seperates.

6. Add the tomato purée and cook further for 5 minutes.

7. Stir in the chicken stock and cook till the curry thickens. Stir in cream. Remove from heat and keep aside.

8. On a serving platter, spread the cooked rice. Remove the kabab as well as tomato, onion and capsicum quarters and arrange neatly on top of the rice.

9. Pour the curry on top and serve hot, garnished with chopped coriander.

Chicken Badam Pasanda

Chicken cooked with almond paste and finished in a rich creamy curry.

Serves: 4, Preparation time: 15 minutes, Cooking time: 40 minutes

Ingredients:

Chicken, escalopes .... 600 gms	Ginger-garlic paste *(page 13)* .... 15 gms / 1 tbs
Egg, whisked 1	White pepper powder .... 3 gms / ½ tsp
Salt .... 12 gms / 2 tsp	Brown onion paste *(page 13)* .... 30 gms / 2 tbs
Red chilli powder .... 7 gms / 1 ½ tsp	Tomato purée *(page 13)* .... 70 gms / 4 ⅔ tbs
Lemon juice .... 10 gms / 2 tsp	Cream .... 50 gms / 3 ⅓ tbs
Ginger-garlic paste *(page 13)* .... 25 gms / 5 tsp	**For garnishing:**
Oil for frying .... 10 gms / 2 tsp	Garam masala *(page 13)* .... a pinch
Almonds, blanched .... 70 gms / 4 ⅔ tbs	Cream .... 5 gms / 1 tsp
Yoghurt .... 100 gms / ½ cup	Almonds, slivered .... 10 gms / 2 tsp
Butter .... 30 gms / 2 tbs	

Method:

1. For the batter, mix together, egg, salt (1 tsp), red chilli powder (½ tsp), lemon juice and ginger-garlic paste.

2. Flatten out each escalope with a steak hammer and coat with the prepared batter. Refrigerate for 15 minutes.

3. Heat oil in a pan and shallow fry the chicken pieces until golden brown on both sides.

4. Remove from heat, drain excess oil and keep aside.

5. For the curry, grind the almonds to a fine past and blend with yoghurt.

6. Heat oil and butter in a pan, add ginger-garlic paste and sauté for a few seconds. Add yoghurt and sauté, stirring constantly.

7. Stir in the remaining salt and red chilli powder alongwith white pepper powder and cook for a few seconds.

8. Stir in onion paste, tomato purée, cream and sauté for 8-10 minutes. Add chicken pieces to the curry and cook on low heat till the pieces are tender and the curry reduces to half.

9. Remove the chicken pieces from the curry and place neatly on a serving platter, pour the curry on top.

10. Sprinkle garam masala and drizzle cream. Serve hot, garnished with slivered almonds and accompained by any Indian bread. (Picture on page 25).

Murg Chakori

Minced lamb stuffed chicken breasts, marinated in yoghurt, cooked in a tandoor

Serves: 4, Preparation time: 40 minutes, Cooking time: 30 minutes

Ingredients:

Chicken, breasts 8
Lamb, minced .... 250 gms
Black cumin *(shah jeera)* .... 2 gms / $^{1}/_{3}$ tsp
Dry ginger *(sonth)* powder .... 5 gms / 1 tsp
Fennel *(saunf)* powder .... 10 gms / 2 tsp
Cumin *(jeera)* powder .... 5 gms / 1 tsp
Red chilli powder .... 5 gms / 1 tsp
Coriander powder .... 5 gms / 1 tsp
Salt .... 10 gms / 2 tsp
Yoghurt .... 50 gms / 3 $^{1}/_{3}$ tbs

Asafoetida *(heeng)* .... a pinch
Oil .... 200 ml / 1 cup
Water .... 200 ml / 1 cup

For the marinade:
Yoghurt, drained .... 500 gms / 2 ½ cup
Salt to taste
Cream .... 100 ml / ½ cup
Red chilli powder .... 5 gms / 1 tsp
Vinegar .... 8 ml / 1 ½ tsp
Coriander powder .... 5 gms / 1 tsp

Method:

1. Clean the chicken breasts, slit open from one side and flatten. Keep aside.
2. Blend together the lamb mince, black cumin, dry ginger powder, fennel powder, cumin powder, red chilli powder, coriander powder, salt, yoghurt and asafoetida.
3. Divide the mince mixture into even size balls. In a pan, heat oil and water in equal quantities, reduce heat and immerse the balls into the pan. Cover and cook for about 20 minutes.
4. Stuff the prepared '*koftas*' meat balls into the chicken breasts. Place the chicken breasts over silver foil and wrap

firmly. Poach for 15 minutes.
5. Remove from heat and unwrap the chicken breast from the foil and allow to cool.
6. For the marinade, blend yoghurt alongwith salt, cream, red chilli powder, vinegar and coriander powder. Keep aside.
7. Marinate the chicken breasts with the prepared marinade and keep aside for 15 minutes.
8. Skewer the chicken breasts and cook in a tandoor for 5-10 minutes or until golden yellow in colour.
9. Remove from the skewers and serve hot, accompanied by Tandoori roti (Page 95).

Tandoori Kofta

Chicken breasts with an exotic filling roasted in a tandoor or in an oven

Serves: 4, Preparation time: 30 minutes, Cooking time: 30-40 minutes

Ingredients:

Chicken, breasts 8
Chicken, minced .... 225 gms
Fenugreek *(methi)* powder .... 2 gms / $^{1}/_{3}$ tsp
Garam masala *(page 13)* .... 2 gms / $^{1}/_{3}$ tsp
White pepper powder .... 7 gms / 1$^{1}/_{3}$ tsp
Green cardamom *(choti elaichi)* powder ... 5 gms / 1 tsp
Salt to taste
Lemon juice .... 5 ml / 1 tsp
Green chillies, chopped 2

Green coriander, chopped .... 3 gms / ½ tsp
Water .... 1 litre / 5 cups
Yoghurt, drained .... 200 gms / 1 cup
Cream .... 80 gms / 5$^{1}/_{3}$ tbs
Saffron *(kesar)* .... a few strands
Oil .... 30 ml / 2 tbs
Red chilli powder .... a pinch
Ginger-garlic paste *(page 13)* .... 30 gms / 2 tbs

Method:

1. Mix half of the fenugreek powder, garam masala, white pepper powder, green cardamom powder, salt, lemon juice, in the chicken mince. Add green chillis and green coriander. Shape into 8 equal round balls and keep aside for 5 minutes.
2. Beat the chicken breast with hammer and put one ball in each breast. Make a round shape alongwith the breast keeping the wing bone standing straight.
3. Wrap it tightly with aluminium foil like a ball.
4. Boil water in a container and cook the chicken breasts in it covered with a lid for 15 minutes.
5. Drain excess water and place the chicken breasts

under running water for 1 minute.
6. Make a second marinade of remaining lemon juice, yoghurt, cream, saffron, oil, salt, red chilli powder and ginger-garlic paste.
7. Marinate the chicken breasts in the second marinade for 5 minutes.
8. Skewer and roast for about 10 minutes in a hot tandoor or in a hot oven (approx 350° F).
9. Remove from skewers and serve hot, garnished with onion rings and lemon wedges and accompanied by Mint chutney (Page 91). (Picture on page 25).

Tandoori Chicken Chaat

An appetiser of sliced tandoori chicken in a spicy masala with a touch of raw mango

Serves: 4, Preparation time: 10 minutes, Cooking time: 10 minutes

Ingredients:

Tandoori chicken, shredded 2	Onions, finely sliced .... 100 gms / ½ cup
Lemon juice .... 15 ml / 1 tbs	Green chillies, chopped .... 10 gms / 2 tsp
Salt to taste	Green coriander, chopped .... 40 gms / 2 ²/₃ tbs
Red chilli powder .... 2 gms / ¹/₃ tsp	Chaat masala .... 10 gms / 2 tsp
Oil .... 15 ml / 1 tbs	Ginger, chopped .... 5 gms / 1 tsp
Raw green mango .... 100 gms / ½ cup	

Method:

1. Prepare a lemon dressing by mixing together the lemon juice alongwith salt, red chilli powder and oil. Keep aside.
2. Cut the raw mango into strips.
3. In a mixing bowl, add mango, onions, green chillies, green coriander, chaat masala alongwith the shredded chicken and the lemon dressing. Mix well.
4. Remove to a serving bowl and serve immediately, garnished with chopped ginger.

Murg Jugalbandi

Chicken breasts stuffed with a filling of chicken mince mixture in a thick curry

Serves: 4, Preparation time: 15 minutes, Cooking time: 1 hour

Ingredients:

Chicken breasts 8	Cumin *(jeera)* Seeds .... a pinch
For the filling:	Ginger-garlic paste *(page 13)* .... 10 gms / 2 tsp
Chicken, minced .... 200 gms	Salt to taste
Oil .... 10 ml / 2 tsp	Red chilli powder .... 2 gms / ¹/₃ tsp
Mustard *(raee)* seeds .... 2 gms / ¹/₃ tsp	Turmeric *(haldi)* powder .... 3 gms / ½ tsp
Curry leaves .... 2 gms / ¹/₃ tsp	Coriander powder .... 5 gms / 1 tsp
Salt .... 2 gms / ¹/₃ tsp	Yoghurt, whisked .... 50 gms / 3 ¹/₃ tbs
Red chilli powder .... 2 gms / ¹/₃ tsp	Tomato purée *(page 13)* .... 50 gms / 3 ¹/₃ tbs
Garam masala *(page 13)* .... 2 gms / ¹/₃ tsp	Brown onion paste *(page 13)* .... 50 gms / 3 ¹/₃ tbs
Coconut, fresh, grated .... 10 gms / 2 tsp	Water .... 80 ml / 1 cup
Oil for frying	Tomato, diced 1
For the curry:	Green peppercorns .... 4 gms / ¾ tsp
Oil .... 20 ml / 4 tsp	

Method:

1. Clean and wash the chicken breasts. Make deep incisions near the bone of the chicken breast, Keep aside.
2. Heat oil in a pan, add mustard seeds and curry leaves, sauté for a few seconds, add the mince and cook for about 5-6 minutes.
3. Add salt, red chilli powder and garam masala alongwith grated coconut, stir and cook for a few minutes. Remove from heat and keep aside to cool.
4. Stuff the chicken breasts with the prepared mixture. Heat oil in a pan, add 2 chicken breasts at a time and sauté till golden brown on both sides. Remove and keep aside.
5. For the curry, heat oil in a pan, add cumin and sauté for a few seconds, add ginger-garlic paste and sauté for 1 minute.
6. Add salt, red chilli powder, turmeric powder and coriander powder and cook for a minute.
7. Stir in the yoghurt and tomato purée and stir-fry on medium heat, add the brown onion paste and cook till oil leaves the sides. Add water and bring to a boil, simmer and cook till the curry reduces to ¾ th.
8. Add the chicken pieces to the curry and allow to cook for 10-12 minutes. Remove from heat.
9. Carefully lift the chicken pieces from the curry and place onto a serving platter. Pour the curry on top and serve hot, garnished with tomato dices and green peppercorns and accompanied by any Indian bread. (Picture on page 25).

Tangri kabab

Chicken drumsticks cooked in a tandoor, coated with egg and cashewnut mixture.

Serves: 4, Preparation time: 1 hour, Cooking time: 15-20 minutes

Ingredients:

Chicken, drumsticks 12
Ginger-garlic paste *(page 13)* .... 20 gms / 4 tsp
White pepper powder .... a pinch
Salt .... 4 gms / 3/4 tsp
Vinegar .... 5 ml / 1 tsp
Yoghurt .... 250 gms / 1 1/3 cups
Cream .... 150 gms / 2/3 cup
Ginger-garlic paste *(page 13)* .... 30 gms / 2 tbs

White pepper powder .... 2 gms / 1/3 tsp
Garam masala *(page 13)* .... 4 gms / 3/4 tsp
Salt .... 2 gms / 1/3 tsp
Saffron *(kesar)* .... a few strands
Oil for basting
Eggs, whisked 4
Cashewnuts, finely ground .... 75 gms / 5 tbs

Method:

1. Wash and clean the chicken drumsticks. Make 4-5 deep vertical incisions.
2. Mix ginger-garlic paste, white pepper powder, salt and vinegar to make a paste. Coat the drumsticks with this paste and rub into the slits. Refrigerate for 15 minutes.
3. Make a second marinade with yoghurt, cream, ginger-garlic paste, white pepper powder, garam masala, salt and saffron.
4. Marinate the chicken in the prepared marinade and

refrigerate for another 15 minutes.
5. Skewer the drumsticks and roast in a tandoor for 3-5 minutes till half cooked. Remove and hang for 2-3 minutes.
6. Baste with oil and roast till completely cooked.
7. Mix together the ground cashewnut and eggs. Coat the drumsticks and roast again till the egg has coagulated.
8. Remove and serve hot.

Murg Aloo Bukhara

Chicken dumplings stuffed with dried plums in an exotic curry

Serves: 4, Preparation time: 30 minutes, Cooking time: 45 minutes

Ingredients:

For the Dumplings:
Chicken, minced .... 1 kg
Cumin *(jeera)* powder .... 3 gms / 1/2 tsp
Black cumin *(shah jeera)* powder .... a pinch
Black cardamom *(bari elaichi)* powder .... 3 gms / 1/2 tsp
Asafoetida *(heeng)* .... 2 gms / 1/3 tsp
Red chilli powder .... 5 gms / 1 tsp
Fennel *(saunf)* seeds .... 6 gms / 1 tsp
Mustard oil .... 40 gms / 2 2/3 tbs
For the filling:
Dried aloo bukhara 16
For the curry:
Mustard oil .... 100 gms / 1/2 cup
Cloves *(laung)* 4

Red chilli powder .... 16 gms / 1 tbs
Water .... 1½ litre / 7 cups
Green cardamom *(choti elaichi)* 4
Black cardamom *(bari elaichi)* 4
Bay leaves *(tej patta)* 2
Black cumin *(shah jeera)* .... a pinch
Salt .... 16 gms / 1 tbs
Turmeric *(haldi)* powder .... 10 gms / 2 tsp
Black cardamom *(bari elaichi)* powder ... 10 gms / 2 tsp
Fennel *(saunf)* powder .... 6 gms / 1 tsp
Cinnamom *(daalchini)* powder .... 6 gms / 1 tsp
Tomatoes, chopped .... 200 gms / 1 cup
Dry ginger powder *(sonth)* .... 2 gms / 1/3 tsp

Method:

1. For the dumplings, mix together all the ingredients and divide into 16 equal portions.
2. Place one aloo bukhara in the centre of each portion. Shape into balls and keep aside.
3. For the curry, heat mustard oil in a handi *(pot)* till it begins to smoke, add cloves and sauté till they crackle. Reduce heat to low.
4. Add the red chilli powder, allow to infuse, stir in water

and bring to a boil.
5. Add the remaining whole and powdered spices and condiments and bring to a boil. Reduce heat to low and gently add the chicken balls to the simmering curry.
6. Allow to cook for 25-30 minutes till the chicken balls are cooked and the curry thickens. Remove from heat and transfer to a serving dish.
7. Serve hot, accompanied by Tandoori roti *(Page 95)*.

FISH & SEAFOOD

Clockwise from left: Jhinga Mehrunisa (page 43), Saloni Fish
Tikka (page 45), Jhinga Til Tikka (page 43) and Tandoori
Pomfret (page 45).

Jalpari Kabab

Saffron flavoured fish rolls stuffed with prawns

Serves:4, Preparation time: 40 minutes, Cooking time: 20 minutes

Ingredients:

Fish fillets, thin 12
Prawns, shelled, deveined .... 220 gms
Ginger-garlic paste *(page 13)* .... 25 gms / 5 tsp
Mango pickle masala .... 25 gms / 5 tsp
Carom *(ajwain)* seeds .... 2 gms / $^1/_3$ tsp
White pepper powder .... 5 gms / 1 tsp
Garam masala *(page 13)* .... 4 gms / ¾ tsp
Salt to taste

Red chilli powder .... 5 gms / 1 tsp
Lemon juice .... 5 gms / 1 tsp
Oil .... 20 ml / 4 tsp
Yoghurt, drained .... 180 gms / $^3/_4$ cup
Cream .... 30 gms / 2 tbs
Saffron *(kesar)* .... a few strands
Green cardamom *(choti elaichi)* powder .... a pinch
Water .... 1 ltr / 5 cups

Method:

1. Extract juice from ginger-garlic paste and keep aside.
2. Clean the fish fillets and prawns. Pat dry with a cloth.
3. Make a marinade with half of the carom seeds, white pepper powder, garam masala, salt, red chilli powder, lemon juice, extract of ginger-garlic paste, pickle masala and oil.
4. Marinate the fish fillets in the prepared marinade and keep aside for 5 minutes.
5. Prepare second marinade of yoghurt, cream, saffron, green cardamom powder and the remaining half of other ingredients. Keep it aside.
6. Put one fish fillet flat on a table top. Place a prawn at one end of the fillet and roll the fillet. Wrap it tightly with cling wrap or aluminium foil.
7. Boil water in a handi *(pot)* and cook the rolls for 10 minutes keeping the pot covered.
8. Drain the water and place the rolls under running water for 1 minute. Remove the foil.
9. Marinate the rolls in the second marinade for 5 minutes.
10. Skewer the rolls and roast it in hot tandoor or in an oven (approx 300-350°F) for 10 minutes.
11. Remove from skewers, transfer to a serving platter and serve hot, accompanied by Mint chutney (Page 91).

Maccher Jhol

Mustard flavoured bengali fish curry

Serves:4, Preparation time:20 minutes, Cooking time: 40 minutes

Ingredients:

Pomfret .... 900 gms
Turmeric *(haldi)* powder .... 5 gms / 1 tsp
Salt .... 10 gms / 2 tsp
Oil .... for frying
Fenugreek *(methi dana)* seeds .... 2 gms / $^1/_3$ tsp
Cumin *(jeera)* seeds .... 3 gms / ½ tsp
Bayleaves *(tej patta)* 4
Onions, finely chopped .... 200 gms / 1 cup

Ginger-garlic paste *(page 13)* .... 20 gms / 4 tsp
Tomatoes, finely chopped .... 100 gms / ½ cup
Green chillies, sliced .... 10 gms / 2 tsp
Red chilli powder .... 4 gms / $^3/_4$ tsp
Coriander powder .... 6 gms / 1 $^1/_3$ tsp
Water .... 500 ml / 2 ½ cups
Green coriander, chopped .... 5 gms / 1 tsp

Method:

1. Wash and clean the fish, remove the head and tail and cut into pieces.
2. Apply half of turmeric powder and salt on the fish pieces and keep aside.
3. Heat oil in a pan and shallow fry the fish on both sides till ¾ done. Remove and keep aside.
4. In the same pan, add fenugreek and cumin seeds, sauté till they crackle, add bayleaves, onions and stir-fry to a golden brown colour on medium heat.
5. Add the ginger-garlic paste, stir-fry for a minute, add tomatoes and cook till the oil separates.
6. Add green chillies, remaining salt, red chilli powder and coriander powder.
7. Cook on a low heat for 2-3 minutes, increase heat, add water and bring to a boil.
8. Add the fish pieces and simmer.
9. Cover and cook for 10-15 minutes, till the fish is completely cooked and the curry has thickened.
10. Remove from heat onto a serving dish and serve hot, garnished with chopped coriander. (Picture on page 38).

Prawn Malai Curry

Sea fresh prawns cooked in a lip smacking curry

Serves: 4, Preparation time: 10 minutes , Cooking time: 30 minutes

Ingredients:

Prawns, shelled, deveined 16	Curry leaves .... *5 gms / 1 tsp*
Coconut, fresh, grated *1*	Salt to taste
Oil .... *50 ml / 3 1/3 tbs*	Yoghurt, whisked .... *50 gms / 3 1/3 tbs*
Ginger-garlic paste *(page 13)* .... *10 gms / 2 tsp*	Tomato purée *(page 13)* .... *50 gms / 3 1/3 tbs*
Red chilli powder....................................... *5 gms / 1 tsp*	Water .... *200 ml / 1 cup*
Coriander powder....................................... *5 gms / 1 tsp*	Garam masala *(page 13)* .... *2 gms / 1/3 tsp*
Turmeric *(haldi)* powder .... *5 gms / 1 tsp*	

Method:

1. Squeeze out the milk from the grate coconut and strain through a muslin cloth. Keep aside.
2. Heat oil in a handi *(pot)*, add all the ingredients except yoghurt and tomato purée. Stir-fry for 2-3 minutes.
3. Stir in the yoghurt and tomato purée, mix well and cook for about 5-7 minutes.
4. Add prawns and stir-fry for 2-3 minutes. Add water to allow the prawns to cook till they are tender and curry thickens, stir in garam masala and coconut milk. Remove from heat and serve, accompanied by steamed rice.

Prawn Mehrunisa

Prawns coated in a rich and creamy marinade, cooked in a tandoor

Serves: 4, Preparation time: 40 minutes, Cooking time: 10 minutes

Ingredients:

Prawns, shelled, deveined .... *1400 gms*	Cheese, grated .... *80 gms / 5 1/3 tbs*
Vinegar .... *40 ml / 2 2/3 tbs*	Dry fenugreek *(kasoori methi)* powder..... *4 gms / 3/4 tsp*
Salt to taste	Ginger-garlic paste *(page 13)* .... *40 gms / 2 2/3 tbs*
Lemon juice .... *20 ml / 4 tsp*	Garam masala *(page 13)* .... *8 gms / 1 1/2 tsp*
Yoghurt... *240 gms / 1 1/3 cup*	Saffron *(kesar)* .... *a few strands*
Cream... *200 gms / 1 cup*	Butter for basting
White pepper powder .... *8 gms / 1 1/2 tsp*	

Method:

1. Wash the prawns with vinegar and salt water. Drain and pat dry.
2. Prepare a marinade by mixing together all the ingredients except butter.
3. Marinate the prawns in the prepared marinade and keep aside for 30 minutes.
4. Skewer the prawns and roast in a moderately hot tandoor for 6-8 minutes. Remove from tandoor and allow excess liquids to drip.
5. Baste lightly with butter and roast again for 2-3 minutes. Remove from skewers and serve, accompanied by Mint chutney (page 91). (Picture on page 39).

Jhinga Til Tikka

Sesame seed coated fried prawns with flavours of Indian spices

Serves: 4, Preparation time: 1 hour, Cooking time: 15 minutes

Ingredients:

Prawns, shelled, deveined .... *1 kg*	Carom *(ajwain)* seeds .... *8 gms / 1 1/2 tsp*
Ginger paste *(page 13)* .... *25 gms / 5 tsp*	Cream .... *60 gms / 4 tbs*
Garlic paste *(page 13)* .... *30 gms / 2 tbs*	Mace *(javitri)* powder................................. *3 gms / 1/2 tsp*
White pepper powder .... *3 gms / 1/2 tsp*	Green cardamom *(choti elaichi)* powder .. *2 gms / 1/3 tsp*
Red chilli powder...................................... *3 gms / 1/2 tsp*	Blackgram *(chana)* roasted, powdered .... *30 gms / 2 tbs*
Salt to taste	Eggs *4*
Lemon juice .... *60 ml / 4 tbs*	Seasame *(til)* seeds .... *50 gms / 3 2/3 tbs*
Cheese, grated .... *60 gms / 4 tbs*	Oil for frying
Yoghurt, drained .... *120 gms / 1/2 cup*	

Method:

1. Mix together ginger paste, garlic paste, white pepper powder, red chilli powder, salt and lemon juice. Marinate the prawns in this mixture and keep aside for 30 minutes.
2. Mix the cheese into the yoghurt along with all the other ingredients except blackgram powder and sesame seeds. Coat the prawns with the cheese mixture and keep aside for 30 minutes
3. In a separate bowl, mix the blackgram powder and sesame seeds, lightly dust the prawns with this mixture and deep fry in hot oil until golden brown in colour.
4. Remove, drain excess oil and serve hot, accompanied by Coriander chutney (page 89). (Picture on page 39).

Saloni Fish Tikka

Fish cooked in a delightful marinade of Indian spices

Serves: 4, Preparation time: 40 minutes, Cooking time: 15-20 minutes

Ingredients:

Fish, cut into boneless pieces .... 800 gms	Ginger-garlic paste *(page 13)* .... 25 gms / 5 tsp
Salt .... 15 gms / 1 tbs	Yoghurt, drained .... 10 gms / 2 tsp
White pepper powder .... 5 gms / 1 tsp	Vinegar... 150 ml / 3/4 cup
Fenugreek *(methi)* powder .... 3 gms / ½ tsp	Cream... 100 gms / ½ cup
Turmeric *(haldi)* powder .... 3 gms / ½ tsp	Mustard oil.. 60 ml / 4 tbs
Red chilli powder................................... 8 gms / 1 ½ tsp	Cloves 16
Garam masala *(page 13)* .... 2 gms / 1/3 tsp	Charcoal piece, live 1
Clove *(laung)* powder .... a pinch	Oil for basting

Method:

1. Wash, clean and dry the fish pieces.
2. Prepare a marinade by mixing together salt, white pepper powder, dry fenugreek powder, turmeric powder, red chilli powder, garam masala, clove powder, ginger-garlic paste, yoghurt, vinegar and cream.
3. Marinate the fish pieces in the prepared marinade and keep in a bowl.
4. Make a well in the centre and put mustard oil and cloves in it. Place the live charcoal piece in the oil and cover the bowl with a lid. Seal the lid so that the smoke does not escape. Keep aside for 30 minutes.
5. Remove the lid, skewer the fish piece and roast in a medium hot tandoor for 5-6 minutes. Remove, from the tandoor and allow excess liquids to drip.
6. Baste with oil and roast again for 2 minutes until done. Remove from skewers and transfer to a serving platter.
7. Serve hot, accompanied by a green salad and Coriander chutney (page 89).

Tandoori Pomfret

Whole pomfret marinated in fine Indian herbs and cooked in a tandoor

Serves:4, Preparation time: 30 minutes, Cooking time: 10-15 minutes

Ingredients:

Pomfret .... 4 / 1600 gms	Yoghurt, thick .... 500 gms / 2 ½ cups
Ginger-garlic paste *(page 13)* .... 120 gms / 1 1/3 cup	Carom *(ajwain)* seeds .... 6 gms / 1 tsp
Salt .... 20 gms / 4 tsp	Dry fenugreek *(kasoori methi)* powder...... 6 gms / 1 tsp
Red chilli powder..................................... 20 gms / 4 tsp	Oil for basting
Garam masala *(page 13)* .... 12 gms / 2 1/3 tsp	

Method:

1. Discard the fins from the pomfrets. Clean the stomach and wash the fish thoroughly.
2. Make incisions ½ " apart on both sides of the pomfrets.
3. Mix together half of ginger-garlic paste, salt, red chilli powder and garam masala. Rub this mixture onto the fish and the slits. Keep aside for 15-20 minutes.
4. Prepare a marinade by mixing the remaining half of ginger-garlic paste, salt, red chilli powder and garam masala alongwith yoghurt, carom seeds and dry fenugreek powder. Marinate the pomfrets in the prepared marinade.
5. Skewer the pomfrets and roast in a medium hot tandoor for 8-10 minutes. Remove from tandoor and allow excess liquids to drip.
6. Brush with oil and roast again for 5-7 minutes.
7. Remove from skewers and serve immediately, garnished with onion rings and lemon wedges and accompanied by Mint chutney (page 91). (Picture on page 39).

L A M B

Clockwise from left: Shahi Shikampuri Kabab (page 51),
Sakhat Kabab (page 53), Gosht ki Nihari (page 53) and
Laziz Pasliyan (page 49)

Baoli Handi

A delicacy of lamb, mushrooms and vegetables cooked in a traditional handi.
Serves: 4, Preparation Time: 20 minutes, Cooking Time: 1 hour

Ingredients:

Lamb, cut into boneless cubes .... *900 gms*	Coriander powder .... *8 gms / 1½ tsp*
Oil .... *125 ml / ²/3 cup*	Turmeric *(haldi)* powder .... *5 gms / 1 tsp*
Cinnamon *(daalchini)* sticks 2	Tomato purée, fresh *(page 13)* .... *200 gms / 1 cup*
Cloves *(laung)* 5	Khoya, grated *(page 13)* .... *30 gms / 2 tbs*
Nutmeg *(jaiphal)* 1	Yoghurt .... *50 gms / 3¹/3 tbs*
Green cardamom *(choti elaichi)* 4	Onion paste, browned *(page 13)* .... *40 gms / 2½ tbs*
Ginger-garlic paste *(page 13)* .... *40 gms / 2½ tbs*	Green peas, shelled .... *100 gms / ½ cup*
Onions, chopped .... *200 gms / 1 cup*	Carrots, cut into rounds .... *200 gms / 1 cup*
Salt to taste	Mushroom, stems removed .... *80 gms / ¹/3 cup*
Red chilli powder .... *6 gms / 1 tsp*	Cashewnuts, whole .... *150 gms / ²/3 cup*
Garam masala *(page 13)* .... *4 gms / ³/4 tsp*	Water .... *800 ml / 4 cups*

Method:

1. Heat oil in a handi *(pot)*, add the whole spices and sauté till they crackle, add ginger-garlic paste and sauté for 3-5 minutes.
2. Add the lamb cubes and onions. Cook on medium heat, until moisture dries out. Add salt and all the spices.
3. Stir in tomato purée and cook till it leaves oil.

4. Mix in all the remaining ingredients. Stir for a few seconds and add water.
5. Reduce heat and cook till the lamb pieces are tender and the curry thickens. Remove from heat.
6. Transfer to a serving dish and serve hot, accompanied by Naan (page 95).

Shola Kabab

Spicy and aromatic lamb chunks cooked in tandoor.
Serves: 4, Preparation time: 2 hours, Cooking time: 15-20 minutes

Ingredients:

Lamb, cut into boneless pieces .... *900 gms*	Mustard *(raee)* seeds, crushed .... *a pinch*
Salt .... *16 gms / 1 tbs*	Cumin *(jeera)* seeds, crushed .... *a pinch*
Red chilli powder .... *8 gms / 1½ tsp*	Coriander seeds, crushed .... *a pinch*
White pepper powder .... *a pinch*	Ginger-garlic paste *(page 13)* .... *35 gms / 2¹/3 tbs*
Fenugreek *(methi)* powder .... *a pinch*	Raw papaya, grated .... *60 gms / 4 tbs*
Green cardamom *(choti elaichi)* powder .... *a pinch*	Mustard oil .... *100 ml / ½ cup*
Garam masala *(page 13)* .... *4 gms / ³/4 tsp*	Vinegar .... *20 ml / 4 tsp*
Onion *(kalonji)* seeds, crushed .... *4 gms / ¾ tsp*	Yoghurt .... *100 gms / ½ cup*
Fennel *(saunf)* seeds, crushed .... *a pinch*	Butter for basting .... *20 gms / 4 tsp*

Method:

1. Wash, clean and dry the lamb pieces.
2. Prepare a marinade by mixing together all the ingredients.
3. Marinate the lamb pieces in the prepared marinade and keep aside for 1 hour 30 minutes.

4. Skewer the marinated lamb pieces and roast in a medium hot tandoor for 10-12 minutes.
5. Baste with butter and roast again for 5 minutes. Remove from skewers and serve hot, accompanied by Coriander chutney (page 89). (Picture on page 46).

Laziz Pasliyan

Cashewnut flavoured spicy lamb chops
Serves: 4, Preparation time: 30 minutes, Cooking time: 1 hour

Ingredients:

Lamb chops, cleaned 16	Garam masala *(page 13)* .... *15 gms / 1 tbs*
Clarified butter *(ghee)* / Oil .... *200 gms /1 cup*	Coriander powder .... *15 gms / 1 tbs*
Onions, chopped .... *500 gms / 2½ cups*	Red chilli powder .... *15 gms / 1 tbs*
Green cardamom *(choti elaichi)* 10	Turmeric *(haldi)* powder .... *3 gms / ½ tsp*
Cloves *(laung)* 4	Salt to taste
Cinnammon *(daalchini)* sticks 4	Cashewnut paste .... *100 gms / ½ cup*
Bayleaves *(tej patta)* 2	Yoghurt .... *225 gms / 1¼ cup*
Ginger-garlic paste *(page 13)* .... *30 gms / 2 tbs*	Ginger, julienned .... *20 gms / 4 tsp*
Tomatoes, chopped .... *700 gms / 3½ cups*	Green coriander, chopped .... *20 gms / 4 tsp*

Method:

1. Heat clarified butter/oil in a kadhai *(wok)*, add onions and sauté over medium heat.
2. Add all the ingredients and mix well. Add cashewnut paste, stir-fry until the oil seperates. Stir in the yoghurt.

3. Add lamb chops, cover and cook, stirring occasionally until the lamb chops are tender and curry thickens.
4. Serve hot, garnished with julienned ginger and chopped coriander. (Picture on page 47).

Kallan Kabab

*Skewered rolls of finely chopped lamb liver and kidney covered with chicken mince
and roasted over a charcoal grill*

Serves: 4, Preparation time: 1 hour, Cooking time: 20-25 minutes.

Ingredients:

Lamb, minced .... *250 gms / 1 ¼ cup*	Green chillies, chopped .... *5 gms / 1 tsp*
Lamb kidney, finely chopped .... *125 gms / ²/3 cup*	Chicken, minced .... *500 gms / 2½ cups*
Lamb liver, finely chopped.................. *125 gms / ²/3 cup*	Salt .... *3 gms / ½ tsp*
Salt .... *3 gms / ½ tsp*	White pepper powder .... *3 gms / ½ tsp*
Red chilli powder............................... *4 gms / ¾ tsp*	Garam masala *(page 13)* .... *a pinch*
Garam masala *(page 13)*......................... *2 gms / ¹/3 tsp*	Fenugreek *(methi)* powder .... *a pinch*
Fenugreek *(methi)* powder .... *a pinch*	Ginger-garlic paste *(page 13)* .... *2 gms / ¹/3 tsp*
Ginger-garlic paste *(page 13)* .... *10 gms / 2 tsp*	Green coriander, chopped .... *4 gms / ¾ tsp*
Green coriander, chopped .... *5 gms / 1 tsp*	Butter for basting .... *20 gms / 4 tsp*

Method:

1. Mix together the lamb mince, kidney, liver, salt, red chilli powder, garam masala, fenugreek powder, ginger-garlic paste, green coriander and green chillies. Keep aside.

2. Skewer the lamb mince mixture and roast in a charcoal grill for 8-10 minutes. Remove from the charcoal grill, place skewer upright to allow excess liquids to drip. Keep aside for 3-5 minutes.

3. Meanwhile, mix chicken mince alongwith all the other ingredients.

4. Apply a coating of the chicken mince mixture evenly onto the lamb mince kababs and roast again for 5-6 minutes.

5. Baste with butter and remove the kababs from skewers in 4 equal portions.

6. Serve immediately, accompanied by a green salad and Mint chutney (page 91).

Shahi Shikampuri Kabab

Stuffed minced lamb balls in an exotic curry.

Serves: 4, Preparation time: 45 minutes, Cooking time: 35 minutes

Ingredients:

Lamb, minced .... *500 gms*	Onions, chopped .... *50 gms / 3 ¹/3 tbs*
Water...................................... *400 ml / 2 cup*	Raisins, chopped .... *25 gms / 5 tsp*
Lentils *(chana daal)* .... *50 gms / 3 ¹/3 tbs*	Oil for frying... *250 ml / 1 ¹/3 cup*
Cloves *(laung)* powder .... *2 gms / ¹/3 tsp*	**For the curry:**
Cinnamon *(daalchini)* powder.................. *2 gms / ¹/3 tsp*	Oil .... *15 ml / 1 tbs*
Green cardamom *(choti elaichi)* powder ... *2 gms / ¹/3 tsp*	Cumin *(jeera)* powder .... *a pinch*
Black cardamom *(bari elaichi)* powder .... *2 gms / ¹/3 tsp*	Ginger-garlic paste *(page 13)* .... *10 gms / 2 tsp*
Mace *(javitri)* .... *a pinch*	Salt .... *4 gms / 1 tsp*
Salt .... *4 gms / 1 tsp*	Red chilli powder.................................... *2 gms / ¹/3 tsp*
Red chilli powder............................... *5 gm / 1 tsp*	Turmeric *(haldi)* powder .... *3 gms / ½ tsp*
Ginger-garlic paste *(page 13)* .... *20 gms / 4 tsp*	Coriander powder .... *5 gms / 1 tsp*
Egg, whisked *1*	Yoghurt, whisked.................................... *50 gms / 3¹/3 tbs*
For the filling:	Tomato purée *(page 13)*...................... *50 gms / 3¹/3 tbs*
Green chillies, chopped .... *5 gms / 1 tsp*	Brown onion paste *(page 13)* .... *50 gms / 3¹/3 tbs*
Green coriander, chopped .... *5 gms / 1 tsp*	Almond paste .... *50 gms /3¹/3 tbs*
Ginger, chopped .... *5 gms / 1 tsp*	Water.. *300 ml / 1½ cups*

Method:

1. Heat water in a handi *(pot)*, add the mince, lentils, whole spices, salt, red chilli powder, ginger-garlic paste and cook for 20-25 minutes or till the water dries up. Remove from heat.

2. Mix in the egg and divide into 16 equal portions.

3. For the filling, mix together all the ingredients. Divide into 16 equal portions. Place one portion of filling over one portion of the mince mixture and shape into a ball. Similarly, prepare the other balls.

4. Heat oil in a kadhai *(wok)* and deep fry the balls a few at a time, till golden brown on all sides. Drain excess oil and keep aside.

5. Heat oil in a pan, add cumin and sauté till they crackle, add ginger-garlic paste and stir-fry for a minute. Add salt, red chilli powder, turmeric powder and coriander powder, cook for a minute.

6. Stir in the yoghurt, tomato purée and brown onion paste, cook on medium heat for 3-4 minutes.

7. Add almond paste and cook till oil separates. Add water, bring to a boil and cook till curry reduces to ¾ th.

8. Add the fried kababs to the curry and mix well. Cook for a few minutes. Remove from heat.

9. Transfer onto a serving platter and serve hot, accompanied by any Indian bread. (Picture on page 47).

Sakhat Kabab

Lamb kababs stuffed with cheese, coated with conflour batter and deep fried.

Serves: 4, Preparation time: 40 minutes, Cooking time: 20-25 minutes

Ingredients:

Lamb, minced .... *900 gms*
Salt .... *5 gms / 1 tsp*
White pepper powder .... *a pinch*
Red chilli powder .... *3 gms / ½ tsp*
Fenugreek *(methi)* powder .... *a pinch*
Ginger-garlic paste *(page 13)* .... *30 gms / 2 tbs*
Green chillies, chopped .... *8 gms / 1½ tsp*
Green coriander, chopped .... *15 gms / 1 tbs*

For the filling:
Processed cheese, grated .... *130 gms / ¾ cup*
Green chillies, chopped .... *20 gms / 4 tsp*

For the batter:
Cornflour .... *70 gms / 4 ²/₃ tbs*
Flour .... *70 gms / 4 ²/₃ tbs*
Egg, whisked 1
Vinegar .... *5 ml / 1 tsp*
Salt .... *to taste*
White pepper powder .... *a pinch*
Ginger-garlic paste *(page 13)* .... *8 gms / 1½ tsp*
Water .... *300 ml / 1½ cup*
Oil for frying

Method:

1. Mix the lamb mince alongwith salt, white pepper powder, red chilli powder, garam masala, fenugreek powder, ginger-garlic paste, green chillies, green coriander. Refrigerate for 15 minutes.

2. Mix together the green chillies and cheese. Divide into 16 equal portions.

3. For the batter, mix cornflour alongwith flour, egg, vinegar, salt, white pepper powder, ginger-garlic paste and water.

4. Make 10 cm long kababs with the mince mixture and skewer in 4 equal parts. Roast in a tandoor for 5 minutes and remove. Allow to cool, remove from skewers in 4 pieces each.

5. Slit each kabab lengthwise and stuff the cheese mixture.

6. Dip the stuffed kababs in the prepared batter and deep fry in hot oil until crisp and golden brown in colour.

7. Remove, drain excess oil and serve hot, accompanied by Mint chutney (page 91).

Gosht Ki Nihari

Lamb cooked in a traditional nihari masala on low heat to infuse together the flavours.

Serves: 4, Preparation time: 30 minutes, Cooking time: 1 hour

Ingredients:

Lamb, cut into pieces .... *1 kg*
Oil .... *200 ml / 1 cup*
Green cardamom *(choti elaichi)* 10
Black cardamom *(bari elaichi)* 2
Cinnamon *(daalchini)* sticks 2
Cloves *(laung)* 5
Nutmeg *(Jaiphal)* 1
Ginger-garlic paste *(page 13)* .... *20 gms / 4 tsp*
Red chilli powder .... *5 gms / 1 tsp*
Turmeric *(haldi)* powder .... *5 gms / 1 tsp*
Salt .... *10 gm / 2 tsp*
Onion paste *(page 13)* .... *200 gms / 1 cup*
Brown onion paste *(page 13)* .... *50 gms / 3²/₃ tbs*

For the curry:
Nihari Masala
Har /Baheda/Amla *(trifla)*
Dry ginger powder *(sonth)*
Fennel *(saunf)* seeds .... *5 gms / 1 tsp*
Cumin *(jeera)* seeds
Coconut
Garam masala *(page 13)* .... *5 gms / 1 tsp*
Tomato purée, fresh *(page 13)* .... *150 gms / ³/₅ cup*
Water .... *600 ml / 3 cup*
Khoya, grated *(page 13)* .... *15 gms / 1 tbs*
Chickpea powder, roasted .... *80 gms / 5¹/₃ tbs*
Saffron *(kesar)* .... *a few strands*

Method:

1. Wash, clean and dry the lamb pieces.

2. Heat oil in a pan, add green cardamom, black cardomon, cinnamon, cloves and nutmeg. When they crackle, stir in the ginger-garlic paste, red chilli powder, turmeric powder and salt, stir fry for 4-5 minutes.

3. Add onion paste and cook on low heat stirring constantly. Sprinkle a little water as and when required. Cover and cook for 15-20 minutes.

4. Stir in the brown onion paste, nihari masala and garam masala, stir-fry till the oil seperates.

5. Add water, khoya and chickpea powder.

6. Add the lamb pieces along with saffron, cover and cook on very low heat for 25-30 minutes or till the lamb pieces are tender and the curry thickens.

7. Remove from heat, transfer to a serving bowl and serve hot.

VEGETARIAN

Clockwise from left: Gobhi Mussallam (page 59), Dhokla (page 61), Hara Kabab and Daal Kabab (page 65) and Baida Kabab (page 63).

Paneer Akbari

Stuffed home made cheese chunks in a creamy tomato curry

Serves: 4, Preparation time: 20 minutes, Cooking time: 35 minutes

Ingredients:

Cottage cheese *(paneer*)* .... *600 gms*

For the Filling:
Khoya *(page 13)* ....*20 gms / 4 tsp*
Cottage cheese* *(paneer)*, mashed .... *30 gms / 2 tbs*
Cashewnuts, chopped ....*10 gms / 2 tsp*
Pickle masala *(any)* ....*5 gms / 1 tsp*
Tomato purée, thick *(page 13)* ....*20 gms / 4 tsp*

For the Batter:
Cornflour ....*50 gms / 3¹/₃ tbs*
Salt ....*3 gms / ½ tsp*
Yellow colour ....*a pinch*
Water as required

For the Curry:
Oil .... *10 ml / 2 tsp + for frying*
Ginger-garlic paste *(page 13)* ....*10 gms / 2 tsp*
Tomato purée, fresh *(page 13)* .... *500 gms / 2 ½ cups*
Salt ....*5 gms / 1 tsp*
Red chilli powder ....*3 gms / ½ tsp*
White pepper powder ....*a pinch*
Fenugreek *(methi)* powder ....*a pinch*
Garam masala *(page 13)* ....*10 gms / 2 tsp*
Butter ....*10 gms / 2 tsp*
Cream ....*20 gms / 4 tsp*

Method:

For recipe of *paneer* turn to page 13.
1. Cut the paneer into 16 fingers and keep aside.
2. For the filling, mix together khoya, cottage cheese, cashewnuts, pickle masala and tomato purée.
3. Stuff the filling between two cottage cheese fingers.
4. For the batter, mix together cornflour, salt, yellow colour and water.
5. Dip the cottage cheese sandwich in the batter and deep fry in hot oil for 2-3 minutes. Remove, drain excess

oil and keep aside.
6. Heat oil (10 ml) in a pan and sauté ginger-garlic paste for 2-3 minutes. Add tomato purée and cook for 8-10 minutes till it thickens.
7. Add the seasoning and spices. Cook for 3-5 minutes, stir in the butter and cream. Remove from heat.
8. Arrange the fried cottage cheese sandwich on a dish and pour the curry on top.
9. Garnish with cream and serve hot.

Rogani Mushrooms

Mushrooms cooked in a rich onion and tomato curry

Serves: 4, Preparation time: 40 minutes, Cooking time: 30 minutes

Ingredients:

Mushrooms,without stems, boiled .... *600 gms*
Oil ....*100 ml / ½ cup*
Bayleaves *(tej patta)* *4*
Mace *(javitri)* ....*2 gms / ¹/₃ tsp*
Cloves *(laung)* *4*
Green cardamom *(choti elaichi)* *4*
Black cardamom *(bari elaichi)* *4*
Cinnamon *(daalchini)* sticks, small *2*
Ginger-garlic paste *(page 13)* ....*20 gms / 4 tsp*
Tomato purée, fresh *(page 13)* .... *300 gms / 1½ cups*
Salt to taste

Red chilli powder ....*10 gms / 2 tsp*
Turmeric *(haldi)* powder ....*5 gms / 1 tsp*
Coriander powder ....*10 gms / 2 tsp*
Brown onion paste *(page 13)* .... *150 gms / ³/₄ cup*
Yoghurt, whisked ....*50 gms / 3¹/₃ tbs*
Water ....*100 ml / ½ cup*
Garam masala *(page 13)* .... *a pinch*
Green coriander, chopped ....*5 gms / 1 tsp*
Ginger, julienned ....*5 gms / 1 tsp*
Green chillies, julienned ....*5 gms / 1 tsp*

Method:

1. Heat oil in a handi *(pot)*, add bayleaves, mace, cloves, green cardamom, black cardamom and cinnamom, sauté till they crackle.
2. Stir in ginger-garlic paste dissolved in a little water and stir-fry till the water dries out.
3. Add tomato purée, salt, red chilli powder, turmeric powder, coriander powder and sauté for 2-3 minutes till the oil seperates.

4. Add the brown onion paste and yoghurt, stir-fry for 2-3 minutes, add the mushrooms alongwith water. Cook on low heat until the curry thickens and the mushrooms are cooked. Remove from heat and transfer to a serving dish.
5. Serve hot, garnished with garam masala, green coriander, julienned ginger and green chillies. (Picture on page 54).

Gucchi Paneer Keema

A delicacy of black mushrooms and cottage cheese stir-fried

Serves: 4, Preparation time: 20 minutes, Cooking time: 20-25 minutes

Ingredients:

Black mushrooms *(Gucchi)* .... 50 gms / 3 ¹/3 tbs
Cottage cheese* *(paneer)* cut to cubes 500 gms/2 ½ cups
Oil .... 40 ml / 2 ²/3 tbs
Cumin *(jeera)* seeds .... 4 gms / ³/4 tsp
Onions, chopped .... 35 gms / 2 ¹/3 tbs
Ginger, chopped .... 10 gms / 2 tsp
Green chillies, chopped .... 5 gms / 1 tsp

Tomatoes, chopped .... 60 gms / 4 tbs
Salt to taste
Red chilli powder .... 4 gms / ³/4 tsp
Turmeric *(haldi)* powder .... 2 gms / ¹/3 tsp
White pepper powder .... 2 gms / ¹/3 tbs
Green coriander, chopped .... 5 gms / 1 tsp

Method:

*For receipe of *Paneer* turn to page 13.
1. Wash and soak the black mushrooms in water for 15 minutes. Drain and chop finely. Keep aside.
2. Heat oil in a pan, add cumin and sauté for a few seconds. Add onions and sauté till light brown, add ginger, green chillies, and tomatoes and stir-fry for 3-4 minutes.

3. Stir in seasoning and the remaining spices. Add the black mushrooms and cottage cheese. Cook on low heat until the cottage cheese and black mushrooms are completely done, stirring constantly. Remove from heat.
4. Transfer to a serving dish, garnish with chopped coriander and serve hot, accompanied by any Indian bread.

Gobhi Mussallam

Spiced whole cauliflower baked in an oven to keep the flavours alive

Serves: 4, Preparation time: 10-15 minutes, Cooking time: 30 minutes

Ingredients:

Cauliflower, floret only .... 175 gms
Turmeric *(haldi)* powder .... a pinch
Salt .... 10 gms / 2 tsp
Bayleaves *(tej patta)* 4
Oil .... 30 ml / 2 tbs
Cloves *(laung)* 4
Green cardamom *(choti elaichi)* 4
Ginger-garlic paste *(page 13)* .... 10 gms / 2 tsp
Water as required
Butter .... 40 gms / 2 ²/3 tbs

Salt to taste
Garam masala *(page 13)* .... a pinch
Red chilli powder .... a pinch
White pepper powder .... a pinch
Cashewnut paste .... 40 gms / 2 ²/3 tbs
Yoghurt .... 40 gms / 2 ²/3 tbs
Tomato purée, fresh *(page 13)* .... 50 gms / 3 ¹/3 tbs
Brown onion paste *(page 13)* .... 50 gms / 3 ¹/3 tbs
Cream .... 50 gms / 3 ¹/3 tbs

Method:

1. Wash and clean the cauliflower floret.
2. Boil water in a pan, add turmeric powder, salt and bayleaves. Gradually add the cauliflower to this brine solution. Cover cook on meduim heat till ³/4th done.
3. Remove from heat and drain excess water. Transfer the cauliflower to an oven proof dish.
4. Heat oil in a pan, add cloves and green cardamoms, sauté till they crackle. Stir in ginger-garlic dissolved in water (2 tsp). When the water dries out add butter, seasoning and spices.

5. Dissolve the cashewnut paste and yoghurt in water (½ cup) and add to the pan. Cook on low heat till it comes to a boil
6. Stir in the tomato purée and brown onion paste.
7. Cover and cook for about 5 minutes and stir in the cream.
8. Remove from heat and pour over the cauliflower floret.
9. Bake in a moderately hot oven for about 5-10 minutes. Remove from the oven, transfer to a serving dish and serve hot. (Picture on page 55).

Nadru Yakhani

Lotus stems cooked in a tangy yoghurt curry

Serves: 4, Preparation time: 20 minutes, Cooking time: 40 minutes

Ingredients:

Lotus stems .... 800 gms	Cinnamon *(daalchini)* powder .... 2 gms / ¹/₃ tsp
Mustard oil .... 250 ml / 1 ¼ cups	Cumin *(jeera)* powder .... 2 gms / ¹/₃ tsp
Water as required	Salt to taste
Cloves *(laung)* 2	Black cardamom *(bari elaichi)* powder ..... 6 gms / 1 tsp
Green cardamom *(choti elaichi)* 2	Yoghurt, whisked .... 1 kg 500gms / 7 ½ cups
Fennel *(saunf)* powder .... 30 gms / 2 tbs	

Method:

1. Scrape away the skin of the lotus stems. Cut into ½ " long pieces, discarding the ends pieces. Wash and drain.

2. Heat oil in a handi *(pot)* till it starts fuming and deep fry till the stems are half cooked. Remove, drain excess oil and keep aside.

3. Add water alongwith lotus stems in a handi *(pot)*, bring to a boil, add all the spices and stir.

4. Boil continuously on medium heat till the water is reduced to half. Stir in yoghurt, cover and cook further, stirring occasionally till the curry thickens and the lotus stems are tender.

5. Remove from heat, transfer to a serving dish and serve hot, accompanied by steamed rice.

Dhokla

A steamed savory preparation of gramflour

Serves: 4, Preparation time: 45 minutes, Cooking time: 30 minutes

Ingredients:

Gramflour *(besan)* .... 500 gms	Green coriander, chopped .... 50 gms / 3 ¹/₃ tbs
Tartar powder .... 12 gms / 2 ¹/₃ tsp	Coconut, grated .... 120 gms / ½ cup
Water .... 400 ml / 2 cups	Lemons 2
Oil .... 40 ml / 2 ²/₃ tbs	Ginger, chopped .... 10 gms / 2 tsp
Vegetable soda .... 12 gms / 2 ¹/₃ tsp	Salt .... 20 gms / 4 tsp
Cumin *(jeera)* seeds .... 10 gms / 2 tsp	Mustard *(raee)* seeds .... 20 gms / 4 tsp
Green chillies, chopped .... 10 gms / 2 tsp	Green chillies, slit .... 30 gms / 2 tbs

Method:

1. Dissolve tartar powder in water (50 ml).

2. Sieve gramflour in a bowl, add rest of the water to it and mix well to break all lumps. Add oil (1½ tbs), tartar dissloved in water and vegetable soda. Mix well.

3. Pour the gramflour mixture in a flat tray and steam for 15 minutes in a steamer or a double boiler with a lid on top. Remove and cool.

4. Make a fine paste by blending together the cumin seeds, green chillies, green coriander, coconut, juice of two lemons, ginger and salt. Keep aside.

5. Heat the remaining oil in a pan, add the mustard seeds and sauté till they crackle. Add slit green chillies, two cups of water. Bring to a boil and pour this over the cooked dhokla. Keep aside to soak.

6. Slice the dhokla into two portions. Apply the prepared paste evenly on one half and place the other half back on top.

7. Cut into square dices and serve. (Picture on page 55).

Khatte Baigan

Tangy Aubergines

Serves: 4, Preparation time:30 minutes, Cooking time:30 minutes

Ingredients:

Aubergine *(baigan)* .... 800 gms
Tamarind *(imlee)* .... 70 gms / 4 ²/₃ tbs
Mustard oil .... 250 ml / 1 ¼ cup
Cloves *(laung)* 2
Green cardamom *(choti elaich)* 2
Green chillies, slit 4
Red chilli powder .... 20 gms / 4 tsp

Water, hot .... 400 ml / 2 cups
Salt to taste
Turmeric *(haldi)* powder .... *a pinch*
Black cardamom *(bari elaichi)* powder .... 2 gms / ¹/₃ tsp
Fennel *(saunf)* powder .... 30 gms / 2 tbs
Cinnamon *(daalchinni)* powder .... 2 gms / ¹/₃ tsp
Cumin *(jeera)* powder .... 2 gms / ¹/₃ tsp

Method:

1. Clean and cut the aubergines into quarters lengthwise.
2. Soak tamarind in sufficient water. Extract the tamarind juice and discard the seeds.
3. Heat mustard oil in a handi *(pot)* and fry the aubergines till half cooked. Remove, drain excess oil and keep aside.
4. Add cloves and green cardamom in the remaining oil and sauté till they crackle, add green chillies and sauté further for a minutes.

5. Stir in the red chilli powder, water (2 cups), salt, turmeric powder and the remaining spices. Bring to a boil and add the tamarind extract. Cook for 3-5 minutes till the curry begins to thicken.
6. Add the fried aubergines. Cover and cook on low heat till the curry has thickened and the aubergines are tender.
7. Remove from heat, transfer to a serving dish and serve hot, accompanied by a green salad and any Indian bread.

Baida Kabab

Skewered rolls of egg and potatoes, roasted in a charcoal grill

Serves: 4, Preparation time: 30-40 minutes, Cooking time: 10-15 minutes

Ingredients:

Eggs 11
Potatoes, boiled .... 200 gms
Garam masala *(page 13)* .... 2 gms / ¹/₃ tsp
Chaat masala .... 2 gms / ¹/₃ tsp
Breadcrumbs .... 100 gms / ½ cup
Salt .... 8 gms / 1 ½ tsp

Red chilli powder .... 2 gms / ¹/₃ tsp
Ginger, chopped .... 10 gms / 2 tsp
Green chillies, chopped .... 5 gms / 1 tsp
Green coriander, chopped .... 5 gms / 1 tsp
Butter for basting .... 30 gms / 2 tbs

Method:

1. Boil 10 eggs, grate them and keep aside. Mash the boiled potatoes.
2. Mix together the grated eggs and mashed potatoes alongwith garam masala, chaat masala, bread crumbs, salt, red chilli powder, ginger, green chillies, green coriander and the raw egg.
3. Divide this mixture into 5 equal portions

4. Wrap each portion along the length of skewers using wet hands leaving a 2 cm gap between each. Roast for 5-10 minutes.
5. Remove and baste with butter. Roast further for 3-5 minutes or until cooked.
6. Remove from skewers and serve hot, accompanied by Mint chutney (page 91). (Picture on page 55).

Daal Panchmela

Mixed lentil curry

Serves: 4, Preparation time: 15 minutes, Cooking time: 1 hour

Ingredients:

Lentils *(malka masoor daal)* .... 40 gms / 2 ²/3 tbs	Red chilli powder .... 5 gms / 1 tsp
Lentils *(chana daal)* .... 40 gms / 2 ²/3 tbs	Oil .... 35 ml / 2 ¹/3 tbs
Lentils *(dhuli urad daal)* .... 40 gms / 2 ²/3 tbs	Butter .... 15 gms / 1 tbs
Lentils *(arhar daal)* .... 40 gms / 2 ²/3 tbs	Cumin *(jeera)* seeds .... 5 gms / 1 tsp
Lentils *(dhuli moong daal)* .... 40 gms / 2 ²/3 tbs	Ginger, chopped .... 10 gms / 2 tsp
Water as required	Tomatoes, chopped .... 60 gms / 4 tbs
Salt .... 10 gms / 2 tsp	Green coriander, chopped .... 5 gms / 1 tsp
Turmeric *(haldi)* powder .... 4 gms / ³/4 tsp	

Method:

1. Pick, clean and wash the lentils.
2. Put the lentils alongwith water, salt, turmeric powder and red chilli powder in a handi *(pot)* and cook on low heat for 40-45 minutes till the lentils are tender.
3. Remove from heat and keep aside.
4. Heat oil and butter in a pan, add cumin and sauté till they crackle. Add ginger, stir-fry to a light brown colour.
5. Add the tomatoes and sauté for a minute. Stir in the green coriander and remove from heat.
6. Temper the cooked lentils with this mixture and serve hot, accompanied by any Indian bread.

Hara Kabab

Shallow fried medallions of spinach and green peas

Serves: 4, Preparation time: 30 minutes, Cooking time: 20 minutes

Ingredients:

Peas, boiled .... 1 kg	Red chilli powder .... 3 gms / ½ tsp
Spinach *(palak)*, boiled .... 400 gms / 2 cups	Garam masala *(page 13)* .... 3 gms / ½ tsp
Ginger, chopped .... 20 gms / 4 tsp	Chaat masala .... 5 gms / 1 tsp
Green chillies, chopped .... 10 gms / 2 tsp	Breadcrumbs, fresh .... 100 gms / ½ cup
Green coriander, chopped .... 10 gms / 2 tsp	Cornflour .... 50 gms / 3 ¹/3 tbs
Salt to taste	Oil for frying

Method:

1. Mash the peas and blend the spinach without adding any water. Mix the mashed peas, spinach purée, ginger, green chillies, green coriander, salt, red chilli powder, garam masala, chaat masala, breadcrumbs and cornflour thoroughly.
2. Divide into equal portions and shape into medallions.
3. Heat oil in a kadhai *(wok)* to smoking point, deep fry the medallions a few at a time until crisp and golden brown on both sides. Remove and drain excess oil.
4. Arrange neatly on a serving platter and serve hot, accompanied by Coriander chutney *(page 89)*. (Picture on page 55).

Daal Kabab

Spiced lentil cutlets

Serves: 4, Preparation time: 30 minutes, Cooking time: 15 minutes

Ingredients:

Lentils *(makla masoor daal)* .... 300 gms	Red chilli powder .... 2 gms / ¹/3 tsp
Water as required	Chaat masala .... 4 gms / ²/3 tsp
Green chillies, chopped, deseeded .... 5 gms / 1 tsp	Breadcrumbs, fresh .... 50 gms / 3 ²/3 tbs
Green coriander, chopped .... 10 gms / 2 tsp	Cornflour .... 5 gms / 1 tsp
Ginger, finely chopped .... 10 gms / 2 tsp	Garam masala *(page 13)* .... 2 gms / ¹/3 tsp
Salt to taste	Oil for frying

Method:

1. Clean, wash and boil lentils alongwith water in a handi *(pot)* for 15 minutes. Drain and mash the lentils.
2. In a mixing bowl, add the mashed lentils alongwith green chillies, green coriander, ginger, salt, red chilli powder, chaat masala, bread crumbs, cornflour, garam masala and mix well.
3. Divide the mixture into 16 portions and shape into flat round cutlets. Heat oil in a kadhai *(wok)* and deep fry the cutlets, few at a time until crisp and light brown in colour. Remove and drain excess oil.
4. Serve hot, accompanied by Coriander chutney *(page 89)*. (Picture on page 55).

Bhindi Kurkuri

Crunchy Okra

Serves: 4, Preparation time: 20 minutes, Cooking time: 20 minutes

Ingredients:

Okra *(bhindi)* .... *1 kg*
Salt to taste
Red chilli powder .... *5 gms / 1 tsp*
Garam masala *(page 13)* .... *5 gms / 1 tsp*
Dry mango *(amchoor)* powder .... *3 gms / ½ tsp*

Chaat masala .... *3 gms / ½ tsp*
Gramflour *(besan)* .... *45 gms / 3 tbs*
Oil for frying
Ginger, julienned *(optional)* .... *7 gms / 1 ½ tsp*
Green chillies, slit *(optional)* *2*

Method:

1. Snip off both ends of each okra, slice lengthwise into four slices.
2. Spread all sliced okra on a flat dish and sprinkle evenly with salt, red chilli powder, garam masala, mango powder and chaat masala. Mix well to coat okra evenly.
3. Sprinkle gramflour over the okra and mix in so they are coated evenly, preferably without adding any water.
4. Divide the okra into two portions.

5. Heat oil in a kadhai *(wok)* till it is smoking.
6. Fry one portion of the coated okra slices, seperating each lightly with a fork. Do not allow slices to stick to each other.
7. Remove from oil when both sides are crispy and brown in colour. Similarly, fry the other portion.
8. Remove to a serving platter and serve hot. Can be garnished with julienned ginger and slit green chillies.

Tilwale Aloo

Sesame seed coated potato cutlets

Serves: 4, Preparation time: 30 minutes, Cooking time: 25 minutes

Ingredients:

Potatoes, boiled .... *1 kg*
Red chilli powder .... *4 gms / ⅔ tsp*
Salt to taste
Garam masala *(page 13)* .... *2 gms / ⅓ tsp*
Green coriander, chopped .... *10 gms / 2 tsp*
Green chillies, chopped .... *4 gms / ¾ tsp*

Ginger, finely chopped .... *8 gms / 1½ tsp*
Breadcrumbs, fresh .... *50 gms / 3 ⅓ tsp*
Cornflour .... *10 gms / 2 tsp*
Sesame *(til)* seeds .... *75 gms / 5 tbs*
Oil for frying

Method:

1. Peel and mash the boiled potatoes.
2. In a mixing bowl, add the mashed potatoes alongwith red chilli powder, salt, garam masala, green coriander, green chillies, ginger, bread crumbs, cornflour and mix thoroughly.
3. Divide this mixture into 16 equal portions and shape

into flat round cutlets.
4. Coat each cutlet with sesame seeds and deep fry in hot oil till crisp and golden brown in colour. Remove and drain excess oil.
5. Serve hot, accompanied by Mint chutney (page 91). (Picture on page 8).

Lauki Nazakat

Richly stuffed bottle gourd with an exotic curry

Serves: 4, Preparation time: 1 hour, Cooking time: 25-30 minutes

Ingredients:

Bottle gourd *(lauki)* .... 1 / 650 gms
Khoya *(page 13)* .... 50 gms / 3 ¹/₃ tbs
Cottage cheese* *(paneer)* .... 200 gms / 1 cup
Cashewnuts, chopped .... 40 gms / 2 ²/₃ tbs
Melon *(magaz)* seeds .... 30 gms / 2 tbs
Raisins .... 25 gms / 5 tsp
Salt to taste
Red chilli powder .... 3 gms / ½ tsp
Garam masala *(page 13)* .... 2 gms / ¹/₃ tsp
Dough for sealing
Oil for frying
For the curry:
Oil .... 50 gms / 3 ¹/₃ tbs
Cloves *(laung)* 4
Green cardamom *(choti elaichi)* 4

Black cardamom *(bari elaichi)* 4
Cinnamon *(daalchini)* sticks 2
Bayleaves *(tej patta)* 4
Ginger-garlic paste *(page 13)* .... 100 gms / ½ cup
Cashewnut paste .... 100 gms / ½ cup
Yoghurt .... 125 gms / ¹/₃ cup
Brown onion paste *(page 13)* .... 80 gms / 5 ¹/₃ tbs
Tomato purée, fresh .... 180 gms / 1 cup
Salt to taste
Coriander powder .... 12 gms / 2 ¹/₃ tsp
Red chilli powder .... 5 gms / 1 tsp
White pepper powder .... 2 gms / ¹/₃ tsp
Cream .... 100 gms / ½ cup
Vetivier *(kewda)* essence .... 2-3 drops

Method:

For recipe of *Paneer,* turn to page 13.
1. Wash, peel and cut the ends of the bottle gourd to make a hollow tube.
2. For the filling, mix khoya and cottage cheese alongwith cashewnuts, melon seeds, raisins, salt to taste, red chilli powder and garam masala.
3. Stuff the bottle gourd with the prepared filling and seal both ends with dough.
4. Heat oil in a kadhai *(wok)* and deep fry the bottlegourd. Do not allow colour to change. Remove, drain excess oil and keep aside.
5. For the curry, heat oil in a heavy bottomed pan, add cloves, green cardamom, black cardamom, cinnamon and bay leaves, sauté till they crackle.

6. Stir in the ginger-garlic paste dissolved in a little water and stir-fry for a minute.
7. Mix the cashewnut paste in yoghurt and add to the pan. Cook for 5-10 minutes.
8. Add brown onion paste, tomato purée, salt, coriander powder, red chilli powder and white pepper powder. Cover and cook on low heat, stirring continuously till the curry thickens.
9. Stir in cream and vetivier. Remove from heat and discard the bayleaves.
10. Cut the prepared bottlegourd into 1½ inch thick slices and arrange neatly on a serving dish slightly overlapping each other and pour the curry on top.
11. Serve immediately, accompanied by any Indian bread.

Gulgule ki Chaat

Creamed lentil dumplings served with grated radish and spicy green chutney

Serves: 4, Preparation time: 1 hour 15 minutes, Cooking time: 30 minutes

Ingredients:

Lentils *(dhuli moong daal)* .... 200 gms / 1 cup
Lentils *(dhuli urad daal)* .... 50 gms / 3 ¹/₃ tbs
Water .... 125 ml / ¹/₃ cup
Oil for frying
For the Chutney:
Coriander leaves .... 200 gms / 1 cup
Mint leaves .... 50 gms / 3 ¹/₃ tbs
Ginger, chopped .... 30 gms / 2 tbs

Green chillies .... 30 gms / 2 tbs
Lemon 4
Cumin *(jeera)* seeds, powdered .... 2 gms / ¹/₃ tsp
Salt to taste
Water as required
Onions rings .... 60 gms / 4 tbs
White radish, grated .... 120 gms / 1/2 cup
Radish leaves, chopped .... 40 gms / 2 ²/₃ tbs

Method:

1. Soak the lentils for 1 hour. Drain and blend into a smooth paste using water.
2. With the prepared paste make lemon sized dumplings and keep aside.
3. Heat oil in a kadhai *(wok)* and deep fry the dumplings a few at a time till crisp and golden brown. Remove, drain excess oil and keep aside.

4. For the chutney, blend green coriander alongwith mint, ginger, green chillies, juice of 4 lemons, cumin powder, salt and water. Keep aside.
5. Place the dumplings neatly on a serving platter, pour the chutney on top and serve, garnished with onion rings, grated radish and radish leaves. (Picture on page 2).

Paneer Kofta in Spinach Curry

Soft cottage cheese dumplings in a flavourful spinach curry

Serves: 4, Preparation time: 10 minutes, Cooking time: 35 minutes

Ingredients:

Cottage cheese* *(paneer)*, mashed .... *500 gms*
Potatoes, boiled, mashed.................... *250 gms / 1 ¹/₃ tsp*
Cornflour .... *50 gms / 3 ¹/₃ tbs*
Salt ....*4 gms / ¹/₃ tsp*
White pepper powder .... *3 gms / ¹/₂ tsp*
Oil for frying
For the curry:
Spinach *(palak)* .... *1 kg*
Oil .... *50 ml / 3 ¹/₃ tbs*

Garlic, chopped.. *5 gms / 1 tsp*
Tomato purée *(page 13)* .... *100 gms / ¹/₂ cup*
Red chilli powder .... *3 gms / ¹/₂ tsp*
Turmeric *(haldi)* powder .... *3 gms / ¹/₂ tsp*
Coriander powder .... *3 gms / ¹/₂ tsp*
Salt .... *5 gms / 1 tsp*
Water.. *600 ml / 3 cup*
Garam masala *(page 13)* .... *2 gms / ¹/₃ tsp*

Method:

*For recipe of *paneer* turn to page 13.
1. Mix together the mashed cottage cheese and potatoes alongwith cornflour, salt and white pepper powder. Divide the mixture into 16 even sized balls.
2. Heat oil in a kadhai *(wok)* and deep fry the balls a few at a time until golden brown. Remove and keep aside.
3. Boil the spinach and blend to a purée.
4. Heat oil in a handi *(pot)*, add garlic, spinach purée and cook for about 2-3 minutes. Stir in the tomato purée and mix well.

5. Add red chilli powder, turmeric powder, coriander powder and salt. Cook for 4-5 minutes.
6. Add water and bring to a boil. Add the fried cottage cheese balls, reduce heat and allow to simmer for 5-7 minutes. Stir in garam masala and cook till the curry has reduced to half. Remove from heat.
7. Carefully remove the balls *'Koftas'* and place on a serving dish, pour the curry on top and serve hot, accompanied by Naan (page 95).

Besan ka Chila

Gramflour pancakes with an assortment of toppings

Serves: 4, Preparation time: 30 minutes, Cooking time: 30 minutes

Ingredients:

Gramflour *(besan)* .... *150 gms*
Cumin *(jeera)* seeds .... *5 gms / 1 tsp*
Turmeric *(haldi)* powder .... *5 gms / 1 tsp*
Red chilli powder.. *5 gms / 1 tsp*
Salt to taste
Green chillies, chopped .... *5 gms / 1 tsp*

Green coriander, chopped .... *10 gms / 2 tsp*
Water as required
Cottage cheese* *(paneer)*...................... *100 gms / ¹/₂ cup*
Tomatoes, chopped ....,...... *50 gms / 3 ¹/₃ tbs*
Onions, chopped .... *50 gms / 3 ¹/₃ tbs*
Oil

Method:

*For recipe of *paneer*, turn to page 13.
1. Mix gramflour, cumin seeds, turmeric powder, red chilli powder, salt, green chillies, green coriander and water to make a batter of spreading consistency.
2. Cut the cottage cheese into small cubes and mix with onions and tomatoes. Keep aside in a bowl.
3. Heat a flat pan, brush it with oil and spread batter to

make a pancake of 7" diameter, cook until crisp on both sides. Sprinkle a little oil to avoid from sticking to the pan.
4. Sprinkle some of the cottage cheese mixture on top and remove.
5. Repeat till all the mixture is used to make 16 pancakes.
6. Arrange neatly on a serving platter and serve hot, accompanied by Pickle or Coriander chutney (page 89).

DESSERTS

Clockwise from left: Imarti (page 81), Lavang Latika (page 83), Chocolate Mousse (page 79) and Kulfi Falooda (page 81).

Malpua

Shallow fried pancakes, soaked in saffron flavoured sugar syrup

Serves: 4, Preparation time: 45 minutes, Cooking time: 20 minutes

Ingredients:

Toned milk .... *2 litres / 10 cups*
Khoya, grated *(page 13)* .... *50 gms / 3 1/3 tbs*
Flour .... *20 gms / 4 tsp*
Cornflour .... *25 gms / 5 tsp*
Green cardamom *(choti elaichi)* powder .. *3 gms / 1/2 tsp*

For the sugar syrup:
Water .... *250 gms / 1 1/3 cups*

Sugar .... *500 gms / 2 1/2 cups*
Vetivier *(kewda)* essence .... *5 ml / 1 tsp*
Yellow colour .... *3 gms / 1/2 tsp*
Clarified butter *(ghee)* .... *for frying*

For garnishing:
Pistachios, chopped, blanched .... *20 gms / 4 tsp*
Saffron *(kesar)* .... *a few strands*

Method:

1. Boil milk in a kadhai *(wok)* till it reduces to ¼
2. Add khoya and reduce heat to low, stir continuously till the khoya is completely dissolved.
3. Remove from heat onto a mixing bowl and allow to cool. Add flour, cornflour, green cardamom powder and mix thoroughly to make a batter.
4. In a pan, boil water alongwith sugar and cook till it reaches a thread like consistency. Mix in vetivier and yellow colour.
5. Heat clarified butter *(ghee)* in a frying pan. Add one ladle of batter and fry on both sides till golden brown in colour. Remove, drain excess oil and immerse directly into the sugar syrup. Repeat the same process until all the batter is used up.
6. Allow the malpua's to soak in syrup for a few minutes.
7. Remove from the sugar syrup and fold the malpua's into half or triangles. Arrange neatly on a serving platter and serve hot, garnished with pistachios and saffron and accompanied by Rabari (page 77).

Shahi Tukda Nawabi

A royal dessert of slices of rich bread soaked in a thickened flavoured milk, richly garnished

Serves: 4, Preparation time: 15 minutes, Cooking time: 1 hour

Ingredients:

Milk .... *1 litre / 5 cups*
Green cardamom *(choti elaichi)* powder .. *2 gms / 1/3 tsp*
Saffron *(kesar)* .... *a few strands*
Sugar .... *100 gms / 1/2 cup*
Milk bread slices *8*
Clarified butter *(ghee)* .... *200 gms / 1 cup*

For the rabari
Milk .... *2 litres / 10 cups*
Sugar .... *100 gms / 1/2 cup*
Green cardamom *(choti elaichi)* powder .. *2 gms / 1/3 tsp*
Saffron *(kesar)* .... *a few strands*
Almonds, slivered .... *10 gms / 2 tsp*
Pistachios, slivered .... *10 gms / 2 tsp*
Saffron *(kesar)* .... *a few strands*

Method:

1. Heat milk in a thick bottomed pan and bring to a boil. Add the cardamom powder and saffron. Remove from heat and mix in the sugar. Keep aside.
2. Heat clarified butter *(ghee)* in a seperate pan and fry the bread slices lightly. Remove, drain excess clarified butter.
3. Dip the fried bread slices in the prepared milk to immerse completely. Allow to stand for 10-15 minutes.
4. For the rabari: Heat milk in a pan and cook till it reduces to 1/3. Stir in the sugar, cardamom powder and saffron. Remove from heat and keep aside to cool.
5. Carefully lift the bread slices from the milk and place on a serving platter. Pour the rabari on top, garnish with slivered almonds and pistachios and strands of saffron.
6. Serve chilled or at room temperature. (Picture on page 72).

Zauq-e-Shahi

Dumplings of khoya, dipped in sugar syrup

Serves: 4, Preparation time: 45 minutes, Cooking time: 15 minutes

Ingredients:

Khoya, grated *(page 13)* .... 100 gms / ½ cup
Chenna .... 20 gms / 4 tsp
Flour, seived .... 5 gms / 5 tsp
Water .... 1 litre / 5 cups
For the sugar syrup:
Water.. 175 ml / ³/4 cup

Sugar .... 200 gms / 1 cup
Clarified butter *(ghee)* for frying
Saffron *(kesar)* .... a pinch
Pistachios, blanched, chopped .... 20 gms / 4 tsp
Rabari *(recipe given below)*

Method:

1. Gently mix the khoya, chenna and flour into a soft smooth dough with a little water. Divide the dough into 20 equal portions. Shape into round balls and keep aside.
2. Heat water in a pan, add sugar and stir continuously till the sugar is completely dissolved to make a thin sugar syrup. Remove from heat and keep aside.
3. Heat clarified butter in a kadhai *(wok)* on a low heat.

Put all the balls and gently stir to fry evenly on all sides. When the balls rise to the surface increase heat to moderate and cook till dark brown in colour.
4. Remove, drain excess oil and immerse in the sugar syrup. Allow to soak till cool.
5. Spread a layer or rabari on a serving dish, arrange the 'kala jamuns' on top. Garnish with saffron and pistachios and serve cold or at room temperature.

Makhana ki Kheer

Popped lotus seeds cooked in simmering milk flavoured with saffron

Serves: 4, Preparation time: 15 minutes, Cooking time: 40 minutes

Ingredients:

Phool makhana *(popped lotus seeds)* .... 50 gms / 3¹/3 tbs
Oil for frying
Milk .... 1½ litres / 7 cups
Raisins .... 20 gms / 4 tsp
Green cardamom *(choti elaichi)* powder .... a pinch
Mace *(javitri)* powder.. a pinch

Nutmeg *(jaiphal)* powder .... a pinch
Sugar .... 100 gms / ½ cup
Pistachios, slivered .... 7 gms / 1¹/3 tsp
Almonds, blanched, slivered .... 7 gms / 1¹/3 tsp
Cashewnuts, slivered .... 7 gms / 1¹/3 tsp

Method:

1. Clean the popped lotus seeds 'makhanas' and keep aside.
2. Heat oil in a kadhai *(wok)* and deep fry the makhanas on medium heat till crisp and golden brown. Remove from heat and drain excess oil.
3. Crush the fried makhanas with a rolling pin.
4. Heat milk in a seperate kadhai *(wok)* and bring to a boil. Stir in the crushed makhanas, raisins, green

cardamom powder, mace powder and nutmeg powder.
5. Reduce heat and cook for about 20 minutes, stirring constantly till the milk reduces to ³/4th.
6. Stir in the sugar. Remove from heat and transfer to a serving bowl.
7. Serve hot, garnished with slivered pistachios, almonds and cashewnuts.

Rabari

Vetivier and saffron flavoured thickened milk

Serves: 4, Preparation time: 10 minutes, Cooking time: 35 minutes

Ingredients:

Milk .... 1½ litres / 7 cups
Khoya, grated *(page 13)* .... 100 gms / ½ cup
Sugar .... 100 gms / ½ cup
Green cardamom *(choti elaichi)* powder .... a pinch

Saffron *(kesar)* .... a few strands
Pistachios, blanched, chopped .... 20 gms / 4 tsp
Vetivier *(kewda)* water .... 3-4 drops

Method:

1. Heat milk in a kadhai *(wok)*, on moderate heat. Stir continuously till the milk reduces to ¹/5th.
2. Add khoya and cook on very low heat for 2-3 minutes, stirring continuously till the khoya is dissolved.
3. Add the sugar and cardamom powder and stir till sugar

is completely dissolved.
4. Remove from heat and transfer to a serving dish. Allow to cool and refrigerate.
5. Garnish with saffron, pictachios and vetivier and serve.

Badam Halwa

A rich almond delight served, garnished with saffron and pistachios

Serves: 4, Preparation time: 12 hours, Cooking time: 40 minutes

Ingredients:

Almonds .... 500 gm / 2½ cups	Sugar powder .... 125 gms / 3/4 cup
Clarified butter *(ghee)* .... 250 gms / 1 1/3 cups	Saffron *(kesar)* .... a few strands
Milk .... 150 ml / 3/4 cup	Pistachios, blanched, chopped .... 20 gms / 4 tsp

Method:

1. Soak almonds in water overnight. Peel the skin and dry. Blend coarsely without adding any water.
2. Heat oil in a kadhai *(wok)*, add the powdered almonds, stir-fry on low heat till golden brown in colour.
3. Stir in the milk and sugar. When the milk comes to a boil, reduce heat and cook till the milk reduces to half.
4. Remove from heat and cover with a lid. Allow to rest for 5 minutes.
5. Remove onto a serving dish, garnish with saffron and pistachios and serve hot.

Chenna Payas

Rasgulla shaped rasmalai in a curd cheese flavoured rabari, one of the best Indian sweet meats

Serves: 4, Preparation time: 20 minutes, Cooking time: 45 minutes

Ingredients:

Milk .... 2 ½ litres / 12 ½ cups	Sugar .... 50 gms / 3 1/3 tbs
Or Chenna .... 350 gms / 1 3/4 cups	Green cardamom *(choti elaichi)* powder .. 2 gms / 1/3 tsp
Sugar .... 400 gms / 2 cups	Saffron *(kesar)* .... 2 gms / 1/3 tsp
Water .... 300 ml / 1½ cup	Almond, slivered .... 10 gms / 2 tsp
Flour *(maida)* .... 25 gms / 5 tsp	Pistachios, slivered .... 10 gms / 2 tsp
Milk .... 1 litre / 5 cups	Saffron *(kesar)* .... a few strands

Method:

1. Boil milk in a pan and curdle it by adding white vinegar or lemon juice.
2. Remove from heat, drain the whey and mash the curd cheese well. Seperate 300 gms for payas and 50 gms for the dumplings.
3. Prepare the sugar syrup by boiling together sugar and water till it reaches a thread like consistency. Reduce heat to low.
4. For the dumplings, make about 40 dumplings and simmer in sugar syrup till they swell upto double their size. (To aid in swelling, the simmering syrup should be allowed to froth which is possible by adding maida to it before adding the dumplings). Remove the dumplings from the sugar syrup and keep aside.
5. For the payas, cook the curd cheese seperated for the payas in a kadhai *(wok)* on very low heat. Add the sugar and stir continuously to prevent the payas from sticking to the sides. Cook till it begins to leave the sides. Remove from heat and allow to cool.
6. For the rabari, in a kadhai *(wok)*, add milk and cook on medium heat till it reduces to 1/3, add the cardamom powder and saffron. Remove from heat and add sugar, stir till it dissolves completely.
7. Transfer the prepared rabari to the kadhai *(wok)* containing the payas and cook for about 10-12 minutes. Remove from heat and keep aside to cool.
8. Gently fold in the prepared *'rasgoolas'* dumplings into the prepared payas and serve chilled, garnished with almonds, pistachios and saffron.

Chocolate Mousse

Melted chocolate in a fluffy and rich dessert

Serves: 4, Preparation time: 15 minutes, Cooking time: 15 minutes

Ingredients:

Chocolate slab .... 100 gms	Gelatine .... 20 gms / 4 tsp
Cocoa powder .... 100 gms / ½ cup	Cornflour .... 40 gms / 2 2/3 cup
Sugar .... 100 gms / ½ cup	Water.. 500 ml / 2 ½ cups
Cream.. 120 ml / 3/4 cup	Egg, white only 2

Method:

1. Blend together the chocolate slab, cocoa powder, sugar, cream (4 tsp), gelatine, cornflour and water.
2. Cook on low heat till it reaches a sauce-like consistency.
3. Remove from heat and allow to cool. Pass through a muslin cloth and keep aside.
4. Blend in the balance cream and the egg whites. Pour into champagne glasses and keep in a refrigerator to allow to set.
5. Serve chilled with chocolate flakes. (Picture on page 73).

Kulfi

The Indian home made ice cream, very rich and flavourful

Serves: 4, Preparation time: 2 hours, Cooking time: 30 minutes

Ingredients:

Milk .... 1½ litres / 7 cups
Saffron *(kesar)* .... a few strands
Yellow colour .... 2-3 drops
Sugar .... 100 gms / ½ cup

Green cardamom *(choti elaichi)* powder .... a pinch
Pistachios, blanched................................. 20 gms / 4 tsp
Cashewnuts, chopped .... 20 gms / 4 tsp

Method:

1. Soak saffron in 1 tbs water.
2. Heat milk in a kadhai *(wok)*, add yellow colour and cook on medium heat stirring constantly for about 20 minutes till it reduces to ¼ th.
3. Remove the milk from heat and add sugar. Stir till the sugar is completely dissolved.
4. Add the remaining ingredients, mix well and pour the

mixture into kulfi moulds.
5. Keep the moulds in a freezer for 1½ hours to allow to set.
6. Remove from the freezer, dip the bottom of the moulds in hot water for a few seconds. Invert onto a serving plate and serve immediately, accompanied by Falooda.

Falooda

Freshly prepared cornflour vermicelli served with kulfi

Serves: 4, Preparation time: 10 minutes, Cooking time: 15-20 minutes

Ingredients:

Water.. 400 ml / 2 cups
Cornflour .... 100 gms / ½ cup

Yellow colour (optional) .... a few drops

Method:

1. Take water in a kadhai *(wok)*, add the cornflour and mix well. Stir in the yellow colour.
2. Cook on low heat stirring continuously till the mixture thickens and becomes gelatinous. Remove from heat.
3. Pour into a falooda press. Place the press over a container of cold water.

4. Press the mixture out in one continous stream without stopping.
5. Remove the falooda press. Change the cold water and store the falooda in a refrigerator and use as required.
6. If desired falooda can be flavoured with Roohafza/ Vetivier/Rose water.
7. Serve chilled, as an accompaniment to Kulfi.

Imarti

Lentil roundels cooked in clarified butter and seized in saffron flavoured sugar syrup

Serves: 4, Preparation time: 1 hour 15 minutes, Cooking time: 30-40 minutes

Ingredients:

Lentils *(dhuli urad daal)* .... 250 gms / 1¼ cups
Water.. 500 ml / 2½ cups
Refined flour................................. 25 gms / 5 tsp
Cornflour .... 25 gms / 5 tsp
Yellow colour................................ 5 ml / 1 tsp
Clarified butter *(ghee)* .... 750 ml / 3 ¾ cups

For the sugar syrup
Sugar .... 1 kg 250 gms / 6 1/4 cups
Water....................................... 1½ litre / 7 cups
Saffron *(kesar)* .... a few strands
Vetivier *(kewda)* water .... 5 ml / 1 tsp

Method:

1. Wash and soak the lentils in water for 1 hour.
2. Drain the lentils and blend to a coarse paste 'peethi'. Add colour and keep aside.
3. Prepare the sugar syrup by boiling water alongwith sugar for about 20 minutes till it reaches a thread-like consistency. Stir in the saffron and vetivier. Reduce heat to low.
4. Heat the clarified butter in a flat kadhai *(wok)*.
5. Stuff the prepared paste into a cloth piping bag and

pipe out the paste in the kadhai in circles and then overlapping with circles on the borders.
6. Fry for 2-3 minutes on each side until a golden yellow colour is achieved.
7. Remove and immerse directly into the hot sugar syrup. Allow to soak for for 2 minutes.
8. Remove, drain excess syrup and serve hot. (Picture on page 73).

Kujja Kulfi

This home made ice cream is set and served in special earthenware cups

Serves: 4, Preparation time: 2 hours, Cooking time: 30 minutes

Ingredients:

Milk .... *1 litre / 5 cups*
Saffron *(kesar)* .... *a few strands*
Sugar .... *65 gms / 4 1/3 tsp*
Yellow colour .... *2-3 drops*

Green cardamom *(choti elaichi)* powder .... *a pinch*
Cashewnuts, chopped .... *20 gms / 4 tsp*
Pistachios, blanched, chopped .... *15 gms / 1 tbs*

Method:

1. Soak the saffron in 1 tbs water.
2. Heat milk in a kadhai *(wok)* and cook on medium heat for about 20 minutes, stirring constantly till reduced to ¼ th.
3. Remove milk from heat and stir in the sugar till it is completely dissolved.
4. Mix in the soaked saffron, yellow colour, green cardamom powder and the nuts.
5. Fill into earthenware moulds 'kujja', cover with a lid and seal with dough.
6. Place the moulds in a freezer for 1½ hours to allow to set.
7. Remove from the freezer, remove the lid and serve immediately.

Lavang Latika

Clove flavoured stuffed and rolled pancakes deep fried and seized in syrup

Serves: 4, Preparation time: 1 hour, Cooking time: 30 minutes

Ingredients:

Refined flour .... *200 gms / 1 cup*
Saffron *(kesar)* .... *a few strands*
Water .... *60 ml / 4 tbs*
Veg.oil .... *30 ml / 2 tbs*
For the filling:
Khoya, mashed *(page 13)* .... *125 gms / 3/4 cup*
Almonds, slivered .... *20 gms / 4 tsp*
Pistachios, slivered .... *20 gms / 4 tsp*

Clove *(laung)* powder .... *3 gms / ½ tsp*
Sugar, powdered .... *30 gms / 2 tbs*
Cloves *(laung)* *12*
Oil for frying
For the sugar syrup:
Sugar .... *500 gms / 2 ½ cups*
Water .... *700 ml / 3 ½ cups*

Method:

1. Sieve the flour and make a well in the centre.
2. Soak saffron in 1 tbs water for 5 minutes and pour into the well alongwith vegetable oil and mix well.
3. Mix water from time to time and knead to make a hard dough. Cover with a wet cloth and allow to rest for 15 minutes.
4. For the filling, mix together khoya, almonds, pistachios, clove powder and sugar. Divide into 12 equal portions.
5. Boil sugar with water to prepare the sugar syrup.
6. Divide the dough into 12 equal portions and shape into balls. Roll out each of these balls into 6" diameter pancakes.
7. Place one portion of filling in the centre of each pancake and brush the edges with water.
8. Fold the pancakes from the right edge to the centre and press firmly to seal in the filling. Repeat from left edge to give a 2" wide strip.
9. Keeping the folded side out, make a ring with the strip. Brush the edges with water and press firmly to seal, secure with a clove.
10. Shallow fry on very low heat till crisp and golden brown in colour. Remove and drain excess oil.
11. Dip in hot sugar syrup to submerge completely, turning gently if required. Allow to soak for 2-3 minutes. Remove and drain excess syrup.
12. Arrange neatly on a serving platter and serve. (Picture on page 73).

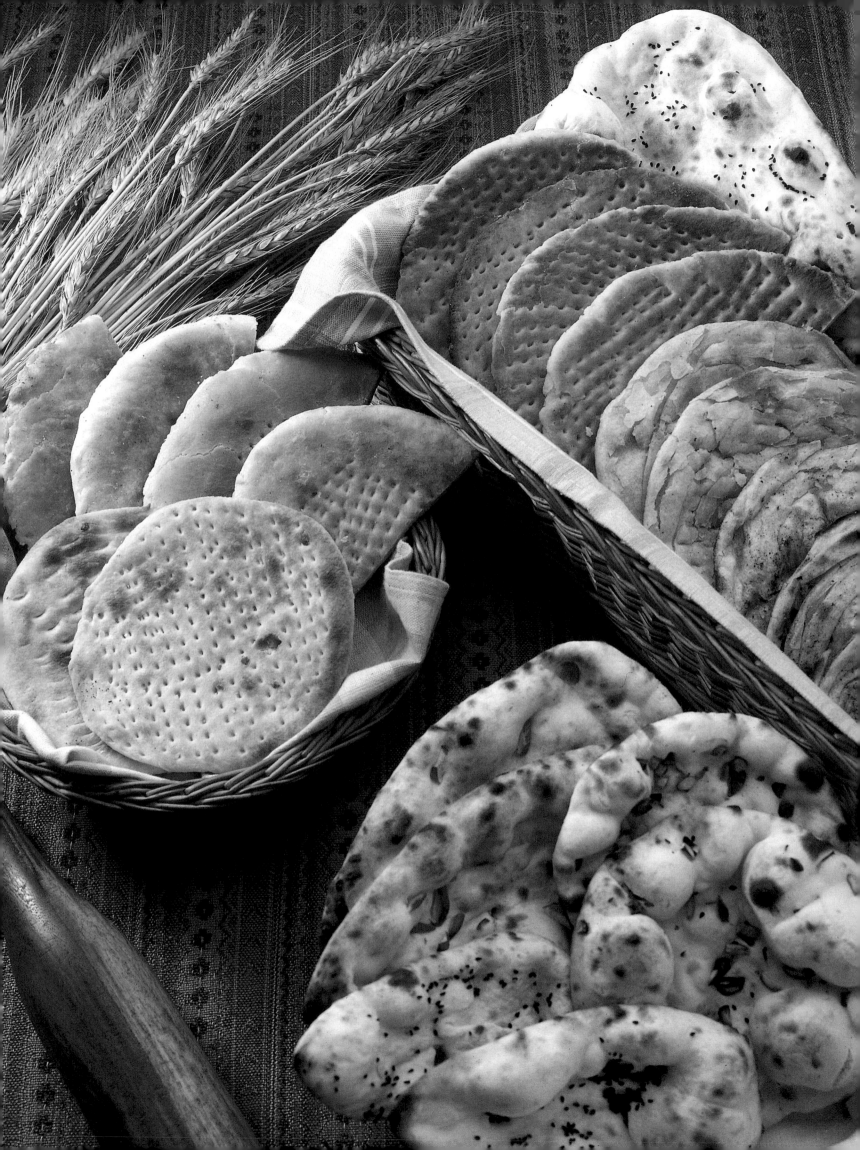

ACCOMPANIMENTS

Clockwise from left: Dahi Bhalla (page 87), Papad, Prawn Biryani and Lamb Biryani (page 94) and Chilman Biryani (page 93).

Dahi Bhalla

Lentil dumplings in a tangy and spiced yoghurt, served with tamarind chutney

Serves: 4, Preparation time: 2 hours, Cooking time: 30 minutes

Ingredients:

For the bhallas:

Lentils *(dhuli urad daal)*	200 gms / 1 cup
Water	600 ml / 3 cups
Salt	2 gms / ¹/₃ tsp
Cumin *(jeera)* seeds	5 gms / 1 tsp
Ginger, chopped	10 gms / 2 tsp
Green chillies, chopped	5 gms
Oil	250 ml / 1 ¹/₃ cup

For the yoghurt mixture:

Yoghurt, thick, whisked	400 gms / 2 cups
Sugar	5 gms / 1 tsp
Salt	2 gms / ¹/₃ tsp
Cumin *(jeera)* seeds, roasted pounded	4 gms / ³/₄ tsp
Black rock salt *(kala namak)*	2 gms / ¹/₃ tsp
White pepper powder	2 gms / ¹/₃ tsp

For garnishing:

Ginger, julienned	5 gms / 1 tsp
Green chillies, julienned	5 gms / 1 tsp
Green coriander, chopped	5 gms / 1 tsp
Red chilli powder	a pinch
Cumin *(jeera)* seeds, roasted, pounded	a pinch
Mint leaves	4 sprigs
Tamarind chutney	40 gms / 2 ²/₃ tbs

Method:

1. Clean the lentils and soak in water for 2 hours. Drain and grind to a fine paste adding a little water if required.
2. Remove onto a mixing bowl and add salt, cumin seeds, ginger, green chillies and mix well. Shape into even sized balls.
3. Heat oil in a kadhai *(wok)*, add the prepared balls, a few at a time using wet hands and deep fry till golden brown in colour. (Make a hole in the centre of the ball with the thumb just before frying). Remove, drain on paper towels.

4. Soak the prepared bhallas in sufficient luke warm water till they are soft.
5. To the whisked yoghurt add sugar, salt, cumin powder, black rock salt and white pepper powder. Mix well.
6. Remove the bhallas from water, squeeze out excess water and add to the yoghurt. Keep aside for 10-15 minutes.
7. Serve chilled, garnished with ginger, green chillies, green coriander, red chilli powder, cumin powder, mint leaves and tamarind chutney.

Kashmiri Mooli ka Raita

A favourite among Kashmiris, grated radish in yoghurt

Serves: 4, Preparation time: 20 minutes

Ingredients:

White radish, grated	350 / 1 ³/₄ cup
Yoghurt, thick	600 gms / 3 cups
Salt	8 gms / 1½ tsp
Green chillies, chopped	8 gms / 1½ tsp
Walnuts, chopped	50 gms / 3¹/₃ tbs

Method:

1. Place the grated radish in a muslin cloth and squeeze out excess water. Remove and keep aside.
2. In a mixing bowl, whisk yoghurt alongwith salt. Add the grated radish, green chillies and walnuts and mix well.
3. Remove onto a serving dish and serve chilled, as an accompaniment to a meal. (Picture overleaf).

Bhindi Raita

Fried okra in yoghurt

Serves: 4, Preparation time: 15 minutes

Ingredients:

Okra *(bhindi)*	100 gms / ½ cup
Oil for frying	
Yoghurt, thick	900 gms / 4 ½ cups
Salt to taste	
Red chilli powder	a pinch
Cumin *(jeera)* seeds, roasted, powdered	a pinch

Method:

1. Wash, clean and dry the okra. Slice them diagonally (2 mm) thick.
2. Deep fry in oil till crisp. Remove and drain excess oil.
3. Whisk yoghurt alongwith salt to taste. Add the fried okra and mix well.
4. Garnish with red chilli powder and cumin powder. Serve chilled, as an accompaniment to a dish. (Picture overleaf).

Boondi Raita

Kashmiri Walnut
Ka Raita

Orange
Raita

Bhindi Raita

Boondi Raita

Crisp small dumplings of gramflour in yoghurt

Serves: 4, Preparation time:30-40 minutes

Ingredients:

Gramflour *(besan)* .... *40 gms / 2½ tbs*
Salt to taste
Baking powder.. *2 gms / ⅓ tsp*
Water as required

Oil for frying
Yoghurt, thick .... *925 gms / 4½ cups*
Cumin *(jeera)* seeds, roasted, crushed .... *a pinch*
Red chilli powder .... *2 gms / ⅓ tsp*

Method:

1. For the Boondi: Mix together the gramflour, salt (¼ tsp) and baking powder in a bowl, gradually add water and whisk to a smooth batter, having consistancy of heavy cream.
2. Heat oil in a deep-frying pan. Pour about 2 tbs of batter at a time into a frying spoon with several holes. Hold the spoon above the pan and press the batter through the holes with your fingers. They will froth in the hot oil, then rise to the surface.

3. Fry until crisp and golden in colour. Remove on paper towels to drain. Repeat the process for all the batter.
4. In a bowl of warm water, put 2-3 tbs of boondis, leave to soften, then gently squeeze between palms to remove excess water, keep aside.
5. Whisk yoghurt alongwith salt to taste, cumin seeds, red chilli powder in a bowl until smooth and creamy.
6. Stir in the soaked boondi and serve at room temperature or chilled, as an accompaniment to any meal.

Orange Raita

Whisked yoghurt served with fresh oranges

Serves: 4, Preparation time: 15 minutes

Ingredients:

Yoghurt, thick .... *925 gms / 4½ cups*
Salt to taste

Oranges .... *200 gms / 1 cup*
Cumin *(jeera)* seeds, roasted, pounded .... *a pinch*

Method:

1. Whisk yoghurt and salt together.
2. Peel, clean and seperate the oranges into segments, cut

into 10 mm squares and add to the yoghurt.
3. Chill and serve, garnished with cumin powder.

Irani Raita

Whisked yoghurt with raisins and honey

Serves: 4, Preparation time: 15 minutes

Ingredients:

Cucumber .... *450 gms*
Yoghurt, whisked .... *800 gms / 4 cups*
Honey .... *80 gms / 5⅓ tbs*
Raisins, chopped .... *40 gms / 2⅔ tbs*

White pepper powder .... *3 gms / ½ tsp*
Salt to taste
Cumin *(jeera)* seeds, roasted, powdered .. *3 gms / ½ tsp*
Green Coriander, chopped........................ *5 gms / 1 tsp*

Method:

1. Peel and chop the cucumbers finely.
2. To the whisked yoghurt add honey, raisins, cucumber, white pepper powder and salt. Mix well.
3. Transfer to a serving bowl and sprinkle cumin powder

and garnish with green coriander.
4. Serve chilled or at room temperature, as an accompaniment to a meal.

Coriander Chutney

A delightful blend of fresh coriander, a must with all kababs

Serves: 4, Preparation time: 20 minutes

Ingredients:

Green coriander, chopped .... *200 gms / 1 cup*
Mint leaves, chopped........................... *50 gms / 3⅓ tbs*
Ginger, chopped .... *30 gms / 2 tbs*
Green chillies, deseeded, chopped *6*

Lemon *1*
Cumin *(jeera)* seeds, pounded .... *3 gms / ½ tsp*
Salt to taste
Water as required

Method:

1. Wash the green coriander and mint leaves thoroughly.
2. Blend green coriander leaves alongwith all the

ingredients to a smooth paste. Transfer onto a serving bowl and serve, as an accompaniment to any dish.

Radish & Walnut
Chutney

Saunth

Tomato
Chutney

Mint
Chutney

Coriander
Chutney

Coconut
Chutney

Coconut Chutney

Freshly grated coconut chutney flavoured with mustard

Serves: 4, Preparation time: 15 minutes

Ingredients:

Coconut, shelled, grated .... *320 gms / 1½ cups*	Lemon .... *½*
Green chillies .... *12 gms / 1¹/₃ tsp*	**For the tempering:**
Ginger, peeled............................ *12 gms / 1¹/₃ tsp*	Oil .... *10 ml / 2 tsp*
Lentils *(chana daal)*, roasted .... *40 gms*	Lentils *(urad daal)*, washed .... *5 gms / 1 tsp*
Water.. *200 ml / 1 cup*	Mustard *(raee)* seeds .... *4 gms / ³/₄ tsp*
Salt to taste	Red chillies, whole *2*

Method:

1. Cut the green chillies and ginger into small pieces. Blend into a smooth paste alongwith coconut, lentils and water. Remove to a bowl.
2. Add salt and juice of half a lemon.

3. Heat oil in a pan, add the lentils, mustard seeds and red chillies, sauté till they crackle. Pour the tempering over the chutney and serve cold, as an accompaniment to any dish.

Mint Chutney

Garden fresh mint paste with yoghurt and spices

Serves: 4, Preparation time: 20 minutes

Ingredients:

Mint, chopped .... *100 gms / ½ cup*	Water.. *20 ml / 4 tsp*
Green coriander, chopped .... *100 gms / ½ cup*	Yoghurt .... *60 gms / 4 tbs*
Cumin *(jeera)* seeds .... *5 gms / 1 tsp*	Dry pomegranate *(anardana)* powder .... *30 gms / 2 tbs*
Ginger, finely chopped............................ *25 gms / 5 tsp*	Salt to taste
Green chillies, finely chopped .... *25 gms / 5 tsp*	Lemon *1*

Method:

1. Wash the green coriander and mint leaves thoroughly.
2. Blend the mint leaves and green coriander alongwith and all the other ingredients except salt and lemon.

3. Transfer to a serving bowl and mix in salt to taste and juice of a lemon. Serve, as an accompaniment to any dish.

Tomato Chutney

Spicy and tangy tomato dip, best savoured with vegetarian snacks

Serves: 4, Preparation time: 10 minutes, Cooking time: 5 minutes

Ingredients:

Tomatoes .... *335 gms / 1³/₄ cup*	Oil .... *10 gms / 2 tsp*
Ginger, chopped .... *8 gms / 1½ tsp*	Lentils *(urad daal)*, washed .... *5 gms / 1 tsp*
Red chilli powder .... *2 gms / ¹/₃ tsp*	Red chillies, whole *1*
Coconut, shelled .... *28 gms / 5 tsp*	Mustard *(raee)* seeds .... *4 gms / ³/₄ tsp*

Method:

1. Blanch the tomatoes by putting in boiling water for a minute. Remove and allow to cool.
2. Blend together the tomatoes, ginger, red chilli powder and coconut to make a purée. Transfer to a serving bowl.

3. Heat oil in a pan, add the lentils, red chillies and mustard seeds, sauté till they crackle.
4. Pour this tempering over the prepared chutney and serve as an accompaniment to any dish.

Yellow Chutney

Roasted gramflour and spices blended together with a distinctive flavour of red chillies and mustard

Serves: 4, Preparation time: 15 minutes

Ingredients:

Black gram *(chana)* .... *200 gms / 1 cup*	Mustard *(raee)* seeds .... *2 gms / ¹/₃ tsp*
Water.. *100 ml / ½ cup*	Curry leaves .... *1 sprig*
Salt to taste	Red chillies, whole *5*
Oil .... *10 ml / 2 tsp*	

Method:

1. Blend black gram with water into a smooth paste. Transfer to a bowl, add salt and mix well.
2. Heat oil in a pan, add mustard seeds and sauté till they

crackle. Add curry leaves and red chillies. Stir and remove from heat. Pour the prepared tempering over the chutney and serve as an accompaniment to any dish.

Chilman Biryani

Lamb biryani cooked on low heat, covered with a rich puff
Serves: 4, Preparation time: 30 minutes, Cooking time: 1 hour 45 minutes

Ingredients:

Lamb, cut into pieces .... *500 gms*
Basmati rice, ... *500 gms / 2½ cups*
Water as required
Mace *(javitri)* powder .... *2 gms / ⅓ tsp*
Green cardamom *(choti elaichi)* *4*
Black cardamom *(bari elaichi)* *4*
Cloves *(laung)* *4*
Bayleaves *(tej patta)* *5*
Oil .... *200 ml / 1 cup*
Onions, sliced .... *50 gms / 3⅓ tbs*
Ginger-garlic paste *(page 13)* .... *25 gms / 5 tsp*

Salt .... *10 gms / 2 tsp*
Red chilli powder .... *10 gms / 2 tsp*
Water .... *1 litre / 5 cups*
Brown onion paste *(page 13)* .... *50 gms / 3⅓ tbs*
Saffron *(kesar)* .... *a few strands*
Vetivier *(kewda)* water .... *10 ml / 2 tsp*
Onions, sliced, browned .... *60 gms / 4 tbs*
For the Chilman *(puff)* covering:
Flour .... *100 gms / ½ cup*
Butter .... *100 gms / ½ cup*
Water .... *75 ml / 5 tbs*

Method:

1. Wash and soak rice in water for 1 hour. Drain and boil in sufficient water alongwith whole spices till ¾ done. Remove from heat, drain and keep aside.
2. Heat oil in a pan, add onion, fry until brown, add ginger-garlic paste with lamb pieces and stir-fry for about 8-10 minutes. Add salt, red chilli powder and water and cook for about 20-25 minutes on medium heat.
3. Stir in the brown onion paste and cook till lamb pieces are tender and the curry thickens. Remove from heat.

4. For the 'chilman' puff covering, mix butter into the flour, add water and knead to a smooth soft dough.
5. In an oven proof handi *(pot)* place alternate layers of rice and lamb curry. Sprinkle saffron, vetvier and onions, browned. Seal the handi *(pot)* with prepared the puff covering and place in a moderately hot oven (150°C-175°C) for 20 minutes or till the covering is cooked.
6. Remove and serve hot, accompanied by Kashmiri Mooli ka Raita (page 87).

Chicken Biryani

Chicken and rice cooked in a flavourful stock, finished on dum
Serves: 4, Preparation time: 1 hour, Cooking time: 1 hour

Ingredients:

Chicken, cut into pieces .... *880 gms*
Basmati rice .... *800 gms*
Oil .... *110 ml / ½ cup*
Ginger-garlic paste *(page 13)* .... *10 gms / 2 tsp*
Water .... *100 ml / ½ cup*
Salt .... *6 gms / 1⅓ tsp*
Green cardamom *(choti elaichi)* *8*
Black cardamom *(bari elaichi)* *8*

Cloves *(laung)* *8*
Cinnamon *(daalchini)* sticks *2*
Black peppercorns .... *1 gm*
Bayleaves *(tej patta)* *4*
Onion, chopped .... *130 gms / 1⅓ cups*
Green chillies, chopped .... *10 gms / 2 tsp*
Yoghurt .... *100 gms / ½ cup*
Chicken stock .... *30 ml / 1½ cups*

Method:

1. Clean, wash and soak the rice for 1 hour.
2. Heat oil (10 ml) in a pan, add chicken pieces, ginger-garlic paste, water and salt (2 gms). Cover and cook on low heat till all the water dries. Remove the chicken pieces and keep aside.
3. Heat oil (100 ml) in a handi *(pot)*, add the whole spices. Sauté till they crackle, add the onions and stir-fry till light brown in colour.
4. Add green chillies and chicken pieces, sauté for a

minutes. Stir in yoghurt, chicken stock and remaining salt. Bring to a boil, stirring continously and reduce heat.
5. Add the drained rice to the pot and stir from time to time till stock has reduced to the level of rice. Cover with a wet cloth.
6. Cook on very low heat (dum) until the rice is cooked and the chicken pieces are tender.
7. Remove from heat, transfer to a serving platter and serve hot, accompanied by Irani raita (page 89).

Saunth

A sweet and tangy concoction of tamarind pulp and spices.
Serves: 4, Preparation time: 15 minutes

Ingredients:

Dry ginger *(sonth)* powder .... *4 gms / ¾ tsp*
Sugar .... *250 gms / 1⅓ cup*
Dry mango *(amchoor)* powder .... *100 gms / ½ cup*
White pepper powder .... *5 gms / 1 tsp*
Red chilli powder .... *10 gms / 2 tsp*

Black rock salt *(kala namak)* .... *5 gms / 1 tsp*
Garam masala *(page 13)* .... *2 gms / ⅓ tsp*
Cumin *(jeera)* powder .... *2 gms / ⅓ tsp*
Fennel *(saunf)* powder .... *2 gms / ⅓ tsp*
Water .... *175 ml / ¾ cups*

Method:

1. Mix together all the ingredients to a smooth paste. Take care to see that no lumps are formed.

2. Strain through a strainer and transfer to a serving dish.
3. Serve cold, as an accompaniment to any dish.

Lamb Biryani

Tender lamb cooked with rice and traditional spices

Serves: 4, Preparation time: 30 minutes, Cooking time: 1 hour 30 minutes

Ingredients:

Lamb, cut into pieces .... *500 gms*
Basmati rice .... *500 gms / 2½ cups*
Water .... *1 litre / 5 cups*
Mace *(jaiphal)* .... *2 gms / 1/3 tsp*
Black cardamom *(bari elaichi)* .... *2 gms / 1/3 tsp*
Green cardamom *(choti elaichi)* .... *2 gms / 1/3 tsp*
Cloves *(laung)* .... *2 gms / 1/3 tsp*
Bayleaves *(tej patta)* *5*
Oil .... *200 ml / 1 cup*

Onions, chopped .... *50 gms / 3 1/3 tbs*
Ginger-garlic paste *(page 13)* .... *25 gms / 5 tsps*
Onion paste, browned *(page 13)* .... *50 gms / 3 1/3 tbs*
Red chilli powder .... *10 gms / 2 tsp*
Salt .... *10 gms / 2 tsp*
Saffron *(kesar)* .... *a few strands*
Vetivier *(kewda) essence .... a few drops*
Onions, chopped, browned .... *50 gms / 3 1/3 tbs*

Method:

1. Clean, wash and soak the rice for 30 minutes. Drain and keep aside.

2. Heat water (750 ml / 3½ cups) in a pot till it comes to a boil, add the rice, mace, black and green cardamoms, cloves and bayleaves. Cover and cook till the rice is 3/4 th done. Remove from heat and keep aside.

3. Heat oil in a pan, and the onions and sauté till light brown in colour. Add the ginger-garlic paste and sauté for a minute.

4. Add the lamb pieces and stir-fry for 10 minutes. Stir in the salt, red chilli powder and water (300 ml / 1½ cups)

cover and cook for 20 - 25 minutes on low heat.

5. Remove the lid, add the brown onion paste and cook further till the lamb pieces are tender and the curry has thickened. Remove from heat and keep aside.

6. In a casserole or a baking dish, place alternate layers of rice and the lamb pieces. Sprinkle saffron and vetivier on top, cover with a wet cloth and cook on very low heat (dum) for 15-20 minutes.

7. Remove from heat, transfer to a serving dish and serve hot, garnished with golden fried onions and accompanied by Boondi raita (page 89). (Picture on page 85).

Prawn Biryani

Fresh prawns cooked with rice in delicate spices and vegetable stock

Serves: 4 , Preparation time: 1 hour, Cooking time: 25 minutes

Ingredients:

Prawns, shelled, deveined .... *100 gms*
Basmati rice ....*350 gms / 1 3/4 cup*
Water .... *400 ml / 2 cups*
Salt to taste
Turmeric powder *(haldi)* .... *a pinch*
Lemon .... *½*
Oil .... *15 ml / 1 tbs*
Cinnamon *(daalchini)* stick *1*
Green cardamom *(choti elaichi)* *4*
Black cardamom *(bari elaichi)* *2*

Cloves *(laung)* *4*
Bayleaves *(tej patta)* *4*
Onions, sliced .... *40 gms / 2 2/3 tbs*
Ginger-garlic paste *(page 13)* .... *10 gms / 2 tsp*
Vegetable stock .... *750 litre / 3 3/4 cup*
Salt .... *8 gms / 1 2/3 tsp*
Butter .... *100 gms / ½ cup*
Lemon *1/2*
Milk .... *50 ml / 3 1/3 tbs*

Method:

1. Pick, wash and soak the rice for ½ hour. Drain and keep aside.

2. Take water in a pan, add salt to taste, turmeric powder and lemon juice. Bring to a boil and add the prawns. Cook till prawns are 3/4 done. Remove, cut into small pieces, keep aside.

3. Heat oil in a handi *(pot)*. Add the whole spices, and sauté till they crackle, add the sliced onions and stir-fry to a golden brown. Add ginger-garlic paste dissolved in a little water.

4. Add the vegetable stock and bring to a boil. Add salt, butter (90 gms) and lemon juice.

5. Add the drained rice and cook on a medium heat, stirring occasionally.

6. When the water has reduced to the level of rice, sprinkle milk on top and cover with a wet cloth.

7. Put on very low heat (dum) for approx 15 minutes or till cooked. Remove from heat.

8. Heat the remaining butter and sauté the prawn pieces for a minute.

9. Transfer the rice to a serving dish and serve hot, garnished with prawns and accompanied by Bhindi raita, (page 87). (Picture on page 85).

Naan

A delicious Royal Indian Bread with a touch of onion and melon seeds

Serves: 4, Preparation time: 3 hours, Cooking time:30 minutes

Ingredients:

Flour *(maida)* ....1 kg	Yoghurt .... 150 gms / 3/4 cup
Salt .... 20 gms / 4 tsp	Water.. 400 ml / 2 cups
Baking powder.............................. 8 gms / 1 ½ tsp	Oil ....20 ml / 4 tsp
Egg, whisked 2	Onion *(kalonji)* seeds .... 5 gms / 1 tsp
Sugar .... 30 gms / 2 tbs	Melon *(magaz)* seeds .... 5 gms / 1 tsp

Method:

1. Mix flour, salt, baking powder, egg, sugar and yoghurt. Add water to knead into a soft and smooth dough.
2. Add oil, knead and punch the dough, cover and keep aside to ferment for 2 hours.
3. Divide the dough into 8 balls, place on a lightly floured surface, sprinkle onion and melon seeds, flatten the balls slightly, cover and keep aside for 5 minutes.

4. Flatten each ball to make a round disc, stretch on one side to form an elongated oval.
5. Place carefully in a tandoor and cook till light brown spots occur on the surface.
6. Remove from the tandoor and serve hot, as an accompaniment to any curry dish. (Picture on page 84).

Tandoori Roti

Unleavened wheat flour pancakes cooked in a tandoor

Serves: 4, Preparation time: 1 hour 15 minutes, Cooking time: 20 minutes

Ingredients:

Whole wheat flour .... 1 kg	Water.. 700 ml / 3 ½ cups
Salt .... 20 gms / 4 tsp	

Method:

1. Seive flour and salt in a mixing bowl. Add water and knead into a smooth and elastic dough. Cover with a moist cloth and keep aside for 1 hour.
2. Place the dough on a floured board. Divide into 16 equal portions and shape into balls. Allow to rest for 5 minutes.

3. Flatten between palms moistened with a little water and oil.
4. Place carefully in a tandoor and cook till light brown in colour.
5. Remove from tandoor and serve, as an accompaniment to any curry dish. (Picture on page 84).

Stuffed Parantha

Spicy potato filling in a leavened whole wheat bread

Serves: 4, Preparation time: 30 minutes, Cooking time: 20 minutes

Ingredients:

Flour.................................... 200 gms / 1 cup	Green chillies, chopped .... 10 gms / 2 tsp
Butter .... 40 gms / 2 2/3 tbs	Green coriander, chopped .... 10 gms / 2 tsp
Water.................................... 80 ml / ½ cup	Salt ....4 gms / 3/4 tsp
For the filling:	Red chilli powder .... 2 gms / 1/3 tsp
Potatoes, boiled, mashed..................... 150 gms / 3/4 cup	Pomegranate *(anardana)* seeds .... 8 gms / 1½ tsp
Ginger, chopped .... 20 gms / 4 tsp	Oil .... 40 gms / 2 2/3 tbs

Method:

1. Mix butter into the flour and knead the flour using water into a smooth pliable dough.
2. For the filling, mix together the potatoes, ginger, green chillies, green coriander, salt, red chilli powder and pomegranate seeds. Divide the filling into 4 equal portions.
3. Divide the dough into 4 equal portions and shape into balls. Flatten each ball between palm and fingers. Place one portion of filling in the centre and seal the edges.

4. Dust with flour and roll out with a rolling pin into a 8" diameter pancake.
5. Heat a tawa *(griddle)*, brush the surface with oil. Place the stuffed parantha on the griddle and cook for a few seconds, brush with oil, turn over and similarly cook on the other side.
6. Both sides of the stuffed parantha should be crisp and delicately browned. Remove and serve immediately, accompanied by any yoghurt preparation.

Index

Great
Indian Recipes

Great
Indian Recipes

Compiled by the Master Chefs of
THE ASHOK GROUP OF HOTELS

Photographs
Deepak Budhraja

Food styling
Preeti Budhraja

TIGER BOOKS INTERNATIONAL
LONDON

This edition published in 1997 by
Tiger Books International PLC
Twickenham

ISBN: 1-85501-905-1

© **Lustre Press Pvt. Ltd. 1997**
M-75 GK II Market, New Delhi-110048, INDIA
Phones: (011) 644 2271/646 2782/0886/0887
Fax: (011) 646 7185
© **Recipes, India Tourism Development Corporation**

Photographer
Deepak Budhraja

Food styling
Preeti Budhraja

Production
N.K. Nigam, Abhijit Raha
Design
Sarita Verma Mathur
Project co-ordinator
Lavinia Rao
Typesetting
Naresh L. Mondal

Printed and bound at
Star Standard Industries Pte. Ltd., Singapore

Acknowledgment

We are grateful for the guidance and cooperation of officers
and staff of the Publicity & Production Division of the
India Tourism Development Corporation, New Delhi
The Ashok Hotel, New Delhi and
Hyderabad House, New Delhi.
Our special thanks to
Mr. Anil Bhandari, Mr. Saleem Hamid, Ms. Chandni Luthra,
Mr. Mahesh Kapoor, Mr. Narendra Piplani
and the Master Chefs
Jaganmoy Chaudhury and Sudhir Sibbal.

**This book is dedicated to all the Master Chefs,
past and present, of the Ashok Group of Hotels, India**

4